I Love Baseball

I Love Baseball

Players, Managers, Sportswriters, and Fans Talk About Their Love for the Game

Wayne Stewart

Foreword by Vern Law

Essex, Connecticut

An imprint of The Globe Pequot Publishing Group, Inc.
64 South Main Street
Essex, CT 06426
www.globepequot.com

Distributed by NATIONAL BOOK NETWORK

British Library Cataloguing in Publication Information available

Library of Congress Cataloging-in-Publication Data available

ISBN 978-1-4930-8531-6 (paper : alk. paper)
ISBN 978-1-4930-8532-3 (electronic)

∞™ The paper used in this publication meets the minimum requirements of American National Standard for Information Sciences—Permanence of Paper for Printed Library Materials, ANSI/NISO Z39.48-1992.

This book is dedicated to my family: Nancy, Sean, Rachel, and Nathan; and Scott and Katie.

And to Bobby Bastock, a great friend who knew more about baseball than 99.9 percent of the people on this planet.

Contents

Foreword

Even before I broke into organized baseball in 1948, I loved baseball. I have also always loved the fact that there are parents who love baseball and pass that love on to their kids.

I loved the era I pitched in for the Pittsburgh Pirates (from 1950 through 1967) when I faced some of the all-time greats like Hank Aaron, Eddie Mathews, and Willie Mays. And people still ask me what my star teammate Roberto Clemente was really like.

And our fans in Pittsburgh cared about baseball and the Pirates, who got involved in the community an awful lot with speaking engagements for Little Leagues and visits to hospitals. They saw we were human, just like everybody else, and that we care about things, especially about our community, about our city, about our family. And for the game of baseball it provided a kind of marriage between the fans and the players. You've got to put a little bit in the box as well as take out of the box, so to speak.

I think it's important for players to stay involved in the community. It's imperative to have a connection with the fans, and not a one-way street that you drive down. When you have that connection, people will respect you and the game.

As a big leaguer, I was, like all of us, competitive. I think all of us like to compete and be a winner—that's another reason to love baseball. I had brothers who played sports and when you're growing up as a kid, why, you're trying to find your place in the world. I found mine.

The game has changed, and I think for the better—except for pitch counts, 100 pitches and you're gone. That's plain nonsense to me (and other competitive players). I want to win my game. I don't want somebody else to win it for me. Back when I played that's the way it was. If a guy is pitching well, let him win the game.

As a kid, I loved all the sports. I played baseball, football, and basketball in high school. A lot of people thought I was better at football than I was at baseball during those years, but I think I chose the right profession. I want to be remembered as someone who loved the game and someone who thought about the fans, the city, and my teammates.

When people first began to talk to me about being a professional player, I thought, "Why not? That's better than digging ditches or picking out weeds from rows, and rows, and rows of corn, and milking cows early in the morning." I worked hard on the farms, and for a dollar a day.

When the movie *Angels in the Outfield* was being made around 1950, a lot of that was filmed in Pittsburgh, but I avoided being in it. I just stayed out of the picture. I didn't want to be a celebrity. I just wanted to be a ballplayer and to be a World Series champion. That was more important than anything else to me. And it still is.

—Vern Law

Introduction

Baseball Has Been Very, Very Good to Me

The title of this book is true. I do love baseball. And I have for many decades, dating back to the 1950s. Because millions of others around the globe also love baseball, it makes sense to explore the many reasons we share this devotion.

The game is a kaleidoscope of unique quirky and classy players, zany and creative team owners, and more. There are also the oddities, the traditions, and the inspirational moments which also make baseball a cornucopia, overflowing with the lore of the diamond which lives on forever.

Personally speaking, I got hooked on baseball at the age of six—and stayed that way through parts or all of eight decades—and it all began in 1956 on the playground of Allen School in my hometown of Donora, Pennsylvania. On the first day of first grade I was wearing a generic baseball cap with a B on it. A kid named Rich Patch who would become a lifelong friend approached me and asked if that letter stood for Brooklyn or the Braves. I had no idea, but when he told me that he liked the Milwaukee Braves, I went along with him, saying something like, "Yeah, this is a Braves cap."

So, now, driven into being a Milwaukee Braves fan in Pittsburgh Pirate territory, I focused on my three idols, Hank Aaron, fellow slugger Eddie Mathews, and ace of the staff, Warren Spahn. It would have made more sense if I was a fan of the St. Louis Cardinals because their legend, Stan Musial, also called Donora his home.

It didn't take long for me to realize that one of the greatest things about baseball is that it can be a surprise party. When you attend a game, you never know what exciting, even record-setting events might unfold.

You might be lucky enough to see a perfect game—not likely, there have only been 22 of them hurled since 1900. Not that lucky? How about a no-hitter? The first one in the modern era was thrown by "Noodles" Hahn in 1900. Since then, 279 additional no-hitters have occurred through 2023. It's still a stretch to figure that you would go to a game and see one of those gems, but how about a nice pitchers' duel, or a fielding spectacle you'll never forget, or even your favorite player hitting a home run? Baseball gives us almost sacred memories to file away in our mental scrapbook.

Becoming a baseball writer was a blessing to a guy who loves the game. I've had the opportunity to go places, do things, and speak with people I otherwise would never have had the chance to meet. I've interviewed 60 Hall of Famers and countless other players. I interviewed a man who threw seven no-hitters, the player I still consider to be the legitimate all-time home-run king, a minor leaguer who once struck out 27 batters in a nine-inning game (Ron Necciai—one of his victims reached first on a wild pitch so there were 28 "outs" in that game). I even got to interview Babe Ruth's daughter and granddaughter.

And, as an aside, it's true a few players were jerks. When I approached Albert Belle in the Cleveland clubhouse, he was playing Ping-Pong before a game. I had interviewed him once before, apparently on one of his good days, so I thought he'd be amenable to having another conversation with me. I was wrong. "Mr. Belle, will you have time later to answer a few questions for me?" He continued to play on, ignoring me. Thinking perhaps he hadn't heard me, I asked again. Just then the Ping-Pong ball bounced near me, so he walked directly in front of me, never as much as giving me a glance. "Mr. Belle?" Nothing. No response from the surly Belle, not even a "Get lost," or an obscenity.

Then there's the self-centered Barry Bonds. A taxi driver told me Bonds once sat in his cab and began puffing on a cigar. When told he had to put the cigar out, Bonds stubbed it out all right—defiantly, on the mat of the taxi's floor.

When I asked Ron Gant if he had a minute to talk with me, he began by uttering two words: "I sure . . ." He paused. Three seconds later he finished his terse sentence, adding one word, "don't." This was not only rude, it was premeditatedly rude.

In 1980, during one of my first years covering games, I was conducting an interview in the Detroit clubhouse using my cumbersome reel-to-reel tape recorder that I had to lug around back then. Out of the corner of my eye I saw Richie Hebner standing nearby, making an obscene gesture mocking me behind my back. At least the Tiger I was interviewing was kind and continued to answer my question.

Now, to dismiss the negative and finally get to my real point here, I want to stress that the *vast* majority of baseball people are considerate, helpful, and very professional. For every Belle and Bonds, there's an Aaron and a Musial.

One of the most enjoyable interviews I ever did was with broadcaster Ernie Harwell, a pleasant, caring person, and a raconteur who shared stories of the old Polo Grounds, of Mickey Mantle, and of many other stars from long ago. The day Hebner mocked me, Harwell saw my plight and came over to me and told me to ignore his immaturity, and encouraged me to continue my career.

Being a baseball writer also opened the door to other interesting experiences. Gregory Schwalenberg, the curator of the Babe Ruth

Museum, was a huge help when I was working on a biography of Babe Ruth. Among other things, he had me put on white gloves, then permitted me to hold a bat used by the Bambino. It was so hefty that when I first lifted it, my hands dipped as if I were holding a heavy, twitching divining rod.

Covering a minor-league game once, the two umpires working that night allowed me to come into their locker room and apply some of the special mud to a baseball, just as all umps do to take the shine off new balls.

Several players have been nice enough to endorse my books with a blurb for the covers such as my old high school baseball teammate Ken Griffey Sr., as well as Vern Law and Elroy Face.

When I wrote my book *1960: When the Pittsburgh Pirates Had Them All the Way*, every Pirate I spoke to via telephone calls was extremely helpful. Quite a few, including that season's Cy Young Award winner, Law, Dick Groat, the 1960 MVP, and Dick Schofield concluded our calls by saying, "Call again anytime."

The first time I interviewed the affable Jim Thome, he asked if I was an out of town reporter. When I said no, he introduced himself to me, prompting me to think, "I *know* who you are, but it's quite modest and friendly of you to provide an introduction."

Three players, Paul Molitor, Doug Drabek, and Rex Hudler, initially told me they were too busy at the moment to talk, but would catch me later. I took their words to be polite brush-offs. I was wrong.

Molitor took batting practice then led me to the dugout bench to chat. After I first approached Drabek on the field, he looked me up later in the clubhouse. As for Hudler, I had asked him if he had any anecdotes that might liven up a book I was working on, *Wits, Flakes, and Clowns: The Colorful Characters of Baseball*. He said he'd think about it and get back to me.

Dale Murphy, like Musial, tremendous with his fans. Came through for the author's sons. WIKIMEDIA COMMONS

I was convinced he would have more important pregame things on his mind, but about 15 minutes later he came up to me: "I thought of something for you," he smiled. More reasons I love baseball.

And here's yet another one. Dale Murphy was the type of man who would go out of his way to pleasantly help others. When I was interviewing him on the field one day, I mentioned that we had something in common—we were both married to women named Nancy and we both had a son named Sean (or Shawn in Murphy's case).

As a few fans began to trickle into the ballpark, I pointed to the stands where my Sean was already seated not too far from the screen behind home plate. I told Murphy that he was my son's favorite player.

Murphy flashed him a smile and hollered a "Hello, Sean," making my son's day.

One year when Murphy was nearing the end of his career, both of my sons, Sean and Scott, wrote separate letters to Murphy, requesting his autograph on Murphy baseball cards they enclosed.

Months and months went by and, though disappointed, they realized not all players take the time to respond to all of their fan mail. Their venture soon was forgotten. However, Murphy was not your typical player. Roughly three years later the mail brought two self-addressed envelopes, easily recognizable by my sons' penmanship. Inside they not only found the autographed cards, but, recalled Scott, "He also included a letter apologizing and explaining that he gets a lot of requests and it took time to return them all." Sean would later give his son Nathan the middle name Murphy.

Another time when I covered a game while also taking my family to the park, Sean was waiting with Nancy at the Will Call window to get their comp tickets. Sean was wearing a Braves uniform, something Vin Scully immediately noticed as he walked by. "Braves, hmmm?," he said with a smile, then tousled my son's hair as a kind gesture to a not-a-Dodgers fan. Baseball is packed with class acts, and Scully is near the top of the list.

When a pitcher named Scott Stewart made it to the majors, I spoke with him and violated the rule stating writers are not to ask players for autographs. Stewart obliged with a unique message: "To Scott Stewart from Scott Stewart." So, just as my dad had once made it possible for me to get Musial's autograph, I was happy to help my sons acquire memorabilia and memories.

I treasure the memories I have from my youth. I'll never forget at least a few details from the first time I ever stepped inside a big-league park, Pittsburgh's Forbes Field. As is the norm for most kids, it was my dad who introduced me to that experience. My first impression after I clicked my way through the turnstile, entered the park's concourse, walked up a ramp leading to the stands, then caught my first glimpse of the lush green diamond below me with the brilliant blue sky and billowy white clouds above is still etched into my memory: I was indoors, yet I was outdoors. It seemed like a pleasurable paradox, a first for me.

Many years later I read an article written by a man who shared his experiences at his first game. His feeling and his words were nearly identical to mine. Fleetingly I thought that my words had been plagiarized. Then, it hit me. I had stumbled across a baseball universal. The awe of being inside a baseball cathedral leaves a lasting impact.

My parents had lost what would have been their first son at birth. With me winding up as an only child, my parents often did their best to spoil me. So it makes sense that while my father didn't exactly love baseball, he *really* loved me.

One time I wanted to see the Pirates host the Braves. I wished for seats near the Braves dugout, naturally more expensive than general admission or bleacher seats. As a steelworker, my dad didn't have tons of expendable money, but he made sure we got those reserved tickets, near the dugout so I could see my three main heroes. Young fans never forget such moments.

My father, who went by his initials, O.J., long before a guy named Simpson came along, had a passing connection with Musial, having grown up in Donora, two blocks away from the Musials. One day, when Stan, then The Boy, approached my dad, who was eight years older than the future Hall of Famer, and asked if he could join the big kids in a game of baseball, he was chased off the field. "You're not good enough to play with us," he was told. In retrospect, how ironic, but yet another baseball memory to cherish.

Author standing by the Stan Musial historical marker in Donora, Pennsylvania, the hometown of both Musial and Stewart. FROM THE AUTHOR'S COLLECTION

Family traditions often involve baseball. My wife, sons, and I often planned our summer vacations to coincide with a baseball date at a ballpark in its inaugural season to accommodate Sean and Scott's desire to see one of the many neoclassical venues which opened during their younger days. One of my son's classmates was a bit envious and called my sons spoiled, but the joy of seeing, for example, stunning Camden Yards, made those allegations tolerable.

Going back two generations, my grandfather loved baseball, too. He listened faithfully to KDKA, the first radio station (and, speaking of baseball families, the broadcaster that day, Harold Arlin, would later have a big-league pitcher for a grandson, Steve Arlin). In turn, my listening to Bob Prince's broadcasts of the Pirate games taught me a great deal about baseball such as the fact that there is a difference between a ground-rule double, specific to the grounds of a given venue, and a book-rule double which, like a ball bouncing over a fence, applies to every ballpark.

One time Prince interviewed team general manager Joe L. Brown, who informed his audience of a fact that's stuck with me forever: The winning team in a large percentage of games will score more runs in one inning than the losing team winds up scoring throughout the entire contest. I've always loved baseball trivia and tidbits like that; something new often pops up, making the sport an endless saga.

Enough about my take on the game—but there's much more to say about the love of baseball. There have been terrific quotes stemming from baseball, tons of movies, songs, and great literature produced about baseball, plus wonderful events and oddities galore to explore. And we'll get into all of that and more as we take a meandering, informal journey through baseball, touching on some topics briefly while taking a deeper, lingering look at others as we rediscover the many reasons we love the game.

Chapter 1

The (Baseball) People Have Spoken

People close to the game, members of the media, celebrity fans, and your ordinary Joe Fan have much to say about the game they adore. No wonder, organized baseball is played—and loved—in around 100 nations and enjoyed by millions of fans across the globe. Naturally, that means people universally want to share their thoughts on the sport.

Over the years, those closest to the game have given us wonderful thoughts about our national pastime. Start with the most popular Chicago player ever, Mr. Cub, Ernie Banks, and his famous quote about his love of baseball. No matter the weather, the Cubs lowly place in the standings, or even if the perpetually pleasant and smiling Banks was feeling a little bit blue, he would bellow out, "Let's play two." Some teammates during the simmering, dog days of summer might cringe at the idea of playing a grueling doubleheader, but not Banks.

Which brings to mind what another slugger, Willie Stargell of the Pittsburgh Pirates commented, "When you start the game, they don't say 'Work ball,' they say, 'Play Ball.'" Roy Campanella had it right when he came up with, "You gotta be a man to play baseball for a living, but you gotta have a lot of little boy in you, too."

Two Yogi Berra lines: "Love is the most important thing in the world, but baseball is pretty good, too." And, "Baseball ain't like football. You can't make up no trick plays." That's not strictly true, but we can let it slide for Yogi.

Earl Weaver put the football comparison another way to illustrate how different the sports are, especially when it comes to schedules and the long grind of baseball: "This ain't a football game, we do this every day." He also compared the two sports when he said, "You can't sit on a lead and run a few plays into the line and just kill the clock. You've got to throw the ball over the damn plate and give the other man his chance. That's why baseball is the greatest game of them all."

The Hall of Fame manager who never made it to the majors as a player, also stated, "Bad ballplayers make great managers, not the other way around. All I can do is help them be as good as they are." And, to

The Hall of Fame, a magnet for baseball fans. A former town mayor compared a visit to the Hall to being in heaven.

a pitcher who was in a very tight spot: "If you know how to cheat, start now." He told another tentative pitcher, "Babe Ruth is dead. Throw strikes."

Some players became philosophical about baseball. Babe Ruth was optimistic, saying, "Every strike brings me closer to the next home run." Bob Feller noted, "Every day is a new opportunity. You can build on yesterday's success or put its failures behind and start over again. That's the way life is, with a new game every day, and that's the way baseball is." Jackie Robinson made an impact with his pioneering play and his words. He once stated, "A life is not important except in the impact it has on other lives."

Some quotes extol defensive play: One line described Tris Speaker and was revived for Willie Mays, stating that their gloves were "where triples go to die." Another line marveled at the glove work of third baseman Pie Traynor. A writer described a batter who "doubled down the left field line, and Traynor threw him out."

Other noteworthy quotes:

> "If my uniform doesn't get dirty, I haven't done anything in the baseball game. —Rickey Henderson
>
> "It's a beautiful day for baseball."—Ernie Banks
>
> "Oh, those bases on balls."—George Stallings
>
> "Baseball is more than a game to me, it's a religion." And, "It ain't nothin' till I call it."—Bill Klem
>
> "Baseball is the champ of them all. Like somebody said, the pay is short and the hours are good."
> —Yogi Berra

"Baseball is the only sport I know that when you're on offense, the other team controls the ball." —Ken Harrelson

"It ain't braggin' if you can do it."—Dizzy Dean

"All I want out of life is that when I walk down the street, folks will say, 'There goes the greatest hitter who ever lived.'"—Ted Williams

"They [the 1927 Yankees] don't just beat you, they break your heart."—Joe Judge

"People ask me what I do in the winter when there's no baseball. I'll tell you what I do. I stare out the window and wait for spring."—Rogers Hornsby

"You just can't beat the person who never gives up." —Babe Ruth

"Playing baseball for a living is like having a license to steal."—Pete Rose

"I could have played baseball another year, but I would have been playing for the money, and baseball deserves better than that."—George Brett

"A person always doing his or her best becomes a natural leader, just by example."—Joe DiMaggio

"I'd like to thank the good Lord for making me a Yankee."—Joe DiMaggio

"Nothing's ever been as fun as baseball." —Mickey Mantle

Ted Williams, the man who wanted to be considered (and arguably may have been) "the greatest hitter who ever lived." COURTESY OF THE LIBRARY OF CONGRESS

"You should shoot for high standards, and believe they're obtainable." —Buster Posey

"I never had a job. I just always played baseball." —Satchel Paige

"The way to make coaches think you're in shape in the spring is to get a tan." —Whitey Ford

"I'm a guy who just wanted to see his name in the lineup every day. To me, baseball was a passion to the point of obsession." —Brooks Robinson

"I am convinced that God wanted me to be a baseball player." —Roberto Clemente

"There is no room in baseball for discrimination. It is our national pastime and a game for all." —Lou Gehrig

"You could be a kid for as long as you want when you play baseball." —Cal Ripken Jr.

"If you're going to play at all, you're out to win. Baseball, board games, *Jeopardy!*, I hate to lose." —Derek Jeter

"Catching a fly ball is a pleasure, but knowing what to do with it after you catch it is a business." —Tommy Henrich

"There are three types of baseball players: those who make it happen, those who watch it happen, and those who wonder what happened." —Tommy Lasorda

"Baseball is like church. Many attend, but few understand." —Leo Durocher

"I really love the togetherness in baseball. That's real true love." —Billy Martin

"Baseball is the only field of endeavor where a man can succeed three times out of ten and be considered a good performer." —Ted Williams

"The greatest feeling in the world is to win a major league game. The second greatest feeling is to lose a major league game." —Chuck Tanner

"Losing is no disgrace if you've given your best." —Jim Palmer

"It's what you learn after you know it all that counts." —Earl Weaver

"Anything you can conceive or believe, you can achieve." —Johnny Sain

"Creating success is tough, but keeping it is tougher. You have to keep producing, you can't ever stop." —Pete Rose

"If what you did yesterday still looks big to you, you haven't done much today." —Wid Matthews

"Stand your ground and take your lumps."
—Yogi Berra

"Luck is the residue of design." —Branch Rickey

"Winning isn't everything. Wanting to win is."
—Catfish Hunter

"Sweat plus sacrifice equals success." —Charlie Finley

"Success has no shortcut, only a high price of pain and humiliation. Baseball requires mental strength."
—Carlton Fisk

"If you don't play to win, why keep score?"
—Vernon Law

"It's like most anything. If you want to be a loser, there's always a way to dwell on the negative. If you want to win, there's always a way to think positively."
—Tony La Russa

"I'm not concerned with your liking or disliking me . . . All I ask is that you respect me as a human being."
—Jackie Robinson

"Scouts would always tell me I was too short, or too heavy, or whatever. But baseball isn't about being a size or a shape. It's about how big you are inside that counts." —Kirby Puckett

Chapter 2

Other Points of View

Great quotes and viewpoints on the game don't flow exclusively from the mouths of baseball people. Some have their origins in movies, books, and quite a few other sources including your ordinary Joe Fan.

Baseball Movie Quotes

A handful of memorable quotes from movies:

> "How can you not be romantic about baseball?" —*Moneyball*
>
> "Man, this is baseball. You gotta stop thinking, just have fun." —*The Sandlot*
>
> "You're killing me, Smalls." —*The Sandlot*
>
> "There's no crying in baseball!" —*A League of Their Own*
>
> "It's supposed to be hard. If it wasn't hard, everyone would do it. The hard is what makes it great." —*A League of Their Own*

"You wanna have a catch?"—*Field of Dreams*

"All I know is when we win a game, it's a team win. When we lose a game, it's a team loss."—*The Bad News Bears*

"Pitcher's got a big butt. Pitcher's got a big butt." —*Rookie of the Year*

"I see great things in baseball. It's our game, the American game. It will repair our losses and be a blessing to us all."—*Bull Durham*

"The only church that truly feeds the soul, day in and day out, is the church of baseball."—*Bull Durham*

"Vaughn has walked the bases loaded on 12 straight pitches. Boy, how can these guys lay off pitches that close?"—*Major League*

"God, I love baseball."—*The Natural*

Miscellaneous Baseball Quotes

Baseball fans, writers, and scholars have captured the game with succinct words, sometimes even fancy words. For instance, some freely use hyperbole to make their points. One classic line describes a strong power hitter like a Harmon Killebrew: "He can hit a ball out of any park, including Yellowstone." Those words immediately conjure up an image of a true slugger.

This game has produced many quotes that convey myriad ideas. Here's a mixed bag of a few:

"Baseball is dull only to dull minds." —Red Barber

"The game itself just turns me on. There's nothing fake about it." —Bob Prince

"Baseball is more than a game. It's like life played out on a field." —Juliana Hatfield

"A hot dog at the game beats roast beef at the Ritz." —Humphrey Bogart

"Baseball, it is said, is only a game. True. And the Grand Canyon is only a hole in Arizona." —George Will

"There are only two seasons: winter and baseball." —Bill Veeck

"You don't save a pitcher for tomorrow. Tomorrow it may rain." —Leo Durocher

"Baseball is a lot like life. It's a day-to-day existence, full of ups and downs. You make the most of your opportunities in baseball as you do in life." —Ernie Harwell

Other Observations on Baseball

Celebrities and baseball people have no monopoly on views and thoughts about baseball. Take the former mayor (2012–2018) of Cooperstown, New York, Jeff Katz, who knew well that a trip to Cooperstown is on every fan's bucket list. "I think there are more reasons for fans coming here than you'd think. There's the, 'I want to visit the Hall of Fame and see the plaques,' but there's also a sense that Cooperstown is this unique setting, which it is. Most people don't experience a place like Cooperstown anymore, most come from cities or suburbs. So a small village where people know each other and where there's still a Main Street feel to things is not something people see from day to day."

Katz was born in Brooklyn in 1962, after the Dodgers had gone west. "Baseball was always the number one sport in conversation—it was always special. There was continuity—my grandfather would talk about going to Ebbets Field in the Thirties, my uncle would talk about going to the Polo Grounds—he was a Giants fan, a family rebel.

"The first time I came to the Hall of Fame, I was almost 11, in 1973. It was just heaven. Like nothing I had ever seen before." That had to be true for a kid who got hooked on baseball around the time the Mets won it all in 1969, "but also I would get a ton of baseball books, like *Willie Mays* by Arnold Hano. Reading about him was so tied to the love of baseball. And I was always a baseball card guy. In a lot of ways the baseball love comes from the love of cards—I collected them before I was watching games."

Bill Oslowski grew up in a house two doors down from where Stan Musial was raised in Donora, Pennsylvania. He recalled, "I used to deliver newspapers with a friend, Joey Poklemba. Our last stop was at a little store where we'd buy a pop and read the local newspaper, the *Valley Independent*. We'd look over the standings and read the box scores. Then we'd play games and try to imitate Roberto Clemente and his stance. That's when I got into baseball."

Douglas Brookbank, who resides in Brevard, North Carolina, grew up in Brooklyn and remains a Dodger fan to this day. His love of baseball began when he was six in 1952. "We played baseball 24 hours a day, sandlot. I got intrigued by statistics and the strategy. As kids we'd debate, 'Why did he bunt? Why didn't he steal?' I was fascinated by that aspect of the game. And the players were very personable—you could actually see them, a Jackie Robinson or a Gil Hodges around town."

As an adult, even after the Dodgers were uprooted and migrated to Los Angeles, Brookbank continued his baseball love affair. "Every morning from April to October, I'd get up and check the Dodgers' box scores before even saying hello to my wife."

Rachel Wells is a reference librarian at the Hall of Fame who first got interested in baseball thanks to her dad. "My father is a huge New York Yankees fan, so growing up I never understood the rules of baseball, but always knew to root for the Yankees."

She theorized why fans flock to the Hall. "The one [main reason] that stands out is that there is truly something for everyone. So many of us have personal relationships with the game of baseball, whether it be watching a game live, rooting for your favorite team, or just playing catch in the backyard growing up.

"Even if someone comes into the Hall of Fame and says that they don't like baseball, they usually end up connecting to something in the Hall, whether it be movies or a piece of pop culture that we have. The National Baseball Hall of Fame and Museum allows people to connect to the game even more than they did before, or maybe for the first time."

Visitors to the library have varied reasons for their trip there. Wells remembered, "I had someone come in who wanted to see information about a player that their father co-wrote about, William 'Dummy' Hoy. I was able to go through our files and find programs as well as some news articles. I was able to watch as they went through the collection and FaceTimed their father, and at the end they said, 'You're making a difference—thank you.' I was incredibly touched."

Another visitor who left an impression on her was David Ortiz. "He was probably the biggest celebrity I had ever met, both physically and figuratively, and he was very kind. Even though I'm a Yankees fan for life, I developed a soft spot for the Red Sox that day."

Scott Townsend, who lives in Cooperstown and works in the Hall of Fame, said, "The main reason I love baseball is because of my grandfather. I really got into it when the Mets picked up Mike Piazza and started playing really well. I see the blue and orange cap of theirs, and I think of my childhood—instantly—how easy it was and how good we had it. It stems from my grandfather. He'd sit and watch games and I'd plop down on the floor with him. We'd watch in silence—how cool childhood can be."

His earliest vivid memories are of the 1988 Mets, but his father and grandfather took him to an exhibition game at Fenway in 1986 when he was just five. "I just remember the pillars obstructing the view and Darryl Strawberry hitting a home run."

What really got him hooked, though, was "how my grandfather talked about really good players like Keith Hernandez's defense or a left-hander's gorgeous swing, like Strawberry's or Curtis Granderson's."

He concluded with a theory about why fans in general love baseball. "Nostalgia is a positive thing. People come through the Hall of Fame, and they always wanted to come here, and then they see the generation of players who got them into the game—they'll see Stan Musial's jersey or Joe DiMaggio's hat. Then they'll wander through and say, 'Wow. Look how the game's changed.' So it reminds them of a simpler time, but they can also still follow the sport and continue to grow as fans with the sport they love. It's also an escape, you can relax—it's nostalgia, leisure, comfort."

Jeremy Sellew is the sports editor of the *Mon Valley Independent* in Monessen, Pennsylvania. He said, "From T-ball to Mustang, Bronco, PONY, and Colt leagues, baseball was always there.

"My parents divorced even before I began playing ball. And while it wasn't the easiest thing to go through, there was something about being on the field that provided comfort and a third home. I realize now that I not only loved baseball, I needed baseball.

"I'd spend the 12-hour trips to the beach in the back of the family van, copying stats from *USA Today* into my own notebook. I hate—no, I loathe math, but love stats. I carried binders of baseball cards, trading cards and looking over statistics with my friends. Afterwards, we'd go to Jefferson playground with our aluminum bats and tennis balls, peppering the neighbor's house with thunderous home runs over the high fence. Those were the best of times.

"As I grew older and away from playing the sport, I made more of an effort to reconnect by attending games at Three Rivers Stadium and now, PNC Park, the most beautiful and best ballpark in our nation.

"While the Pirates continue to break my heart year after year, there's nothing like being in the park on a beautiful, sunny day and just taking in a game. The sights, the sounds, the smells and the crack of the bat. There's just nothing better and nothing like it.

"My love of baseball led me to a love of all sports. It led me to a bachelor's and master's degree in sports management, and ultimately, to the job I have today as a sports editor."

David Ormandy grew up in London, Ontario, where he watched "hockey, curling and the occasional baseball game on TV. My Uncle Jim taught me about sports. He took me to Detroit for my 14th birthday on June 6, 1972, to Tiger Stadium to see the Angels in a twi-night doubleheader. I got to see Mickey Lolich, Nolan Ryan, Al Kaline, Willie Horton, Norm Cash, and more.

"I had never seen a building like Tiger Stadium, before or since. A true sports cathedral. The players flying around, the crack of the bat, the greenness of the grass, and the utter magnitude of the grand old stadium were overwhelming for me. He even let me have a sip of his beer! Thanks to my Uncle Jim, I became hooked on baseball that day. And my love for the National Pastime will never diminish. Every boy should have an uncle like him."

Bobby Bastock of Lorain, Ohio, was an avid baseball fan who loved his Cubbies. A veritable *Macmillan Baseball Encyclopedia*, he was a whiz at trivia. His daughter Ashley summed up why he loved the game so deeply, conjuring up memories of the man.

She began, "There's one picture I always think of when I think of my dad—him standing in the Jacobs Field bleachers, arms outstretched, baseball hat in his right hand, beer in his left, a big smile on his face.

"I know it's how he always wanted to be remembered. Happy. Doing something he loved. My dad loved baseball more than anyone I know. He could find an interesting storyline in any MLB game. He loved a good pitching duel, the puzzle solving aspect of the game.

"He relished the history of the game more than anyone I've ever met too. He was seemingly doing a perpetual rewatch of Ken Burns' *Baseball* documentary. He had more baseball cards than any of us can count. He even taught his then four-year-old daughter to memorize the starting lineup to the 1955 Brooklyn Dodgers—and yes, the names of Pee Wee Reese, Duke Snider, Gil Hodges, Sandy Amoros, Roy Campanella still come to me easily at 31 years old, as does the fact that Jackie Robinson was actually the third baseman on that team.

"These are all the memories I come back to regularly following his death in 2022. My dad's love of baseball and sports in general was a big influence on me becoming a sports reporter. But since he's been gone, his love of the game has helped me remember him how he wanted to be remembered. It's how I choose to see him. In my memories, he's my dad, but he's also a baseball fan who loved the game in its purest form.

"He's the guy with the hat in one hand, beer in the other, just excited to see what that afternoon's game had in store."

Chapter 3

The Name Game

Whether it's the jargon of the game, the nicknames of teams, or of the players, the language of baseball is sweet music.

Older fans and those who have studied the game are familiar with colorful terms and phrases. Begin with slang expressions such as third base being called the hot corner due to the many sizzling grounders that rocket in that direction. And you don't hear the phrase, "The batter took the collar" much any longer—that meant he went hitless, he was "O," as in a circular collar, for x amount of at-bats.

Most fans know what being on deck means, but maybe only older fans know that the batter who would follow the on-deck hitter is said to be "in the hole." The list goes on (feel free to Google any unfamiliar ones): Texas Leaguer, Baltimore chop, Hot Stove League, around the horn double play, twin killing and twinbills, twi-night doubleheader, Punch and Judy hitter, seeing-eye hit, or a ball that "had eyes," a bleeder, a dying quail, worm burner, rhubarb, and candy arm.

There's also the lost art of bench jockeying, the bases being juiced, hose, payoff pitch, purpose pitch, chin music, Uncle Charlie, aspirin tablet, cheese and gas, an outfielder getting on his horse, and tape-measure homers which began with a Mickey Mantle shot literally measured the old-fashioned way at 565 feet.

Some interesting expressions/phrases include a player who was in the majors but only briefly, just long enough to have "a cup of coffee." A pitcher "pulled the string" when he threw a Bugs Bunny changeup, a ball that "found some grass" fell into the outfield for a hit, and a "can of corn" is an easy out flyball.

And there's a Yankee expression originally tied to how they frequently put up runs late in 1927 games at about the time shadows rolled in—that was time for their "five o'clock lightning" to strike. "Take off at the crack of the bat," is simple, yet solid advice. As are, "Hit 'em where they ain't," and "Take two and hit to right." Long ago Branch Rickey preached that "You can't teach speed." Just as everyone knows that "you can't steal first base."

Playing "station-to-station baseball" refers to baserunners playing it cautiously on the bases in certain situations, unwilling to try to go advance, say, first to third on a single. The tools of ignorance means the gear catchers wear, implying one has to be stupid to play that demanding position even though that's positively untrue.

"No doubles defense" is a strategy used when a team is tied or holds a slim lead and is willing to give up a single if it means avoiding giving up a two-base hit that would suddenly put a runner in scoring position. It applies to outfielders' positioning, trying to cut off the gaps, and involves first and third basemen hugging and guarding the foul lines.

Other specific defenses have names. Infielders, for instance, may be stationed at their normal depth, but managers sometimes have their players positioned otherwise, such as being up at the corners, in at second and short, in all the way around, or at double play depth.

Certain teams gained a secondary nickname. For example, in 1971, the Pittsburgh Pirates first took on their identity as the Lumber Company because of hitters who wielded their bats so effectively, mainly Roberto Clemente, Willie Stargell, and Al Oliver. The 1979 Bucs team became the "We Are Family" group headed up by team captain Stargell.

Other examples include the Go Go Sox, referring to the pennant-winning White Sox of 1959, a team which utilized their speed and base burglary to succeed. The Hitless Wonders White Sox dates back to 1906 when they hit .230 as a team, worst in the AL. They hit only seven homers all year long yet won the World Series after somehow finishing third in the league in runs scored.

The youthful 1950 Phillies team won the pennant as the Whiz Kids. The Brooklyn Dodgers of that decade later had the name the Boys of Summer bestowed upon them. Don't forget the Cardinals' group of rough-and-tumble players known in the 1930s as the Gas-house Gang.

The 1927 world champion Yankees led by Babe Ruth and Lou Gehrig were so fearsome they became known as the Murderers' Row squad. Another Yankees nickname, the Bronx Bombers, became popular in 1936, and the team has often been referred to that way ever since.

The New York Mets were dubbed the Amazin' Mets early in their existence, and that became really accurate in 1969 when the once pathetic team (they lost a record 120 games in their inaugural season of 1962) stunned the baseball world when its then obscure pitching staff headed by Tom Seaver helped them upset the Orioles to win it all. Of course, they were also called the Miracle Mets that season, but another team had the miracle label decades before.

In 1914, nothing much was expected of the Boston Braves, who had finished 31 games out of first place the year before. When the 1914 season opened, they began playing the same way they had in the previous season. On the Fourth of July, they were firmly lodged in the cellar,

14 games under .500 and 15 games behind the New York Giants, who couldn't conceive they would tumble below the lowly Braves.

But that happened mainly due to an unfathomable Boston surge. From that day on, two Braves starters went 35-2! They tied the Giants for the top spot in the league on September 5 then soon breezed through their final games. By season's end, they sat atop the NL, resting 35 games above .500 and 11½ games ahead of New York.

OK, said the experts, so they won the NL flag, the Philadelphia Athletics with 99 wins to their credit would put them in their proper place. Boston swept them, proving they deserved to be called the Miracle Braves.

Some interesting minor-league and college nicknames from the past and present: a team in Winston-Salem went by the name of the Carolina Disco Turkeys, another North Carolina team was called the Burlington Sock Puppets, the name Albuquerque Isotopes was a tip of the cap to *The Simpsons*, the Rocket City Trash Pandas played near Huntsville, Alabama, famous for its association with the space program, an alien/UFO theme ties in with the Las Vegas 51s, next come the Jacksonville Jumbo Shrimp, Asheville Moonshiners, Lansing Lugnuts, Toledo Mud Hens, Amarillo Sod Poodles, and a Kentucky team was called the Florence Y'alls.

A few more: Kannapolis Intimidators, Hickory Crawdads, Richmond Flying Squirrels, Chattanooga Lookouts, Akron RubberDucks, Auburn Doubledays, Traverse City Pit Spitters, Omaha Storm Chasers, and, of course, the wild and crazy Savannah Bananas.

Even some ballparks took on nicknames. The House That Ruth Built is, of course, Yankee Stadium, while Hank Aaron's home park in Atlanta was called the Launching Pad. Another famous nickname is the Friendly Confines for Wrigley Field. When the Diamondbacks park was named Bank One Ballpark, that title was shortened to the BOB. The Big A was the home of the Angels in Anaheim, and some people simply called the Giants' Candlestick Park the Stick. The Twins' park, the Hubert H. Humphrey Metrodome, took on the smaller mouthful of the Homerdome. Some fans call Minute Maid Park, with its retractable roof, the Juice Box.

From 1954 through 2003, the player who was listed first among every big leaguer ever was, quite fittingly, Hank Aaron. He was bumped from that position 50 years later by David Aardsma. In 2015, Tony Zych became the man whose last name sits at the bottom of the all-time roster. Among Hall of Famers, the A–Z list runs from Aaron to Robin Yount.

A slew of players have interesting names. For some reason, it seems as if the Montreal Expos (not counting the franchise players who suited up as Washington Nationals) had a disproportionate number of players who make this handpicked list: Boots Day, Razor Shines, Pepe Frías, Coco Laboy (not to be confused with Coco Crisp), and the favorite of the Expos PA man, John ("Bock-a-bell-ah") Boccabella.

Baseball has seen a Dock Ellis, a Doc Gooden, Doc Cramer, Doc Edwards, Doc White, Doc Crandall, and a Doc Medich. In 1976, while pitching for the Pirates and still going through medical school, Medich saved the life of an elderly fan stricken by a heart attack while in the stands by giving him CPR. He repeated his lifesaving act two years later when he was with the Rangers. For the record, there was also a Yankee who became a practicing cardiologist, Bobby Brown.

The family of Vernon Law deserves mention. When naming their six children, his wife VaNita decided to stick with the letter V for a first initial with daughter VaLynda and sons Varlin, Vaughn, Veryl, Veldon, and Vance. Vance went on to play in the majors.

Some players' last names make their nicknames an inevitable choice. Men named Campbell are frequently called Soups, while the surname Rhodes invites the moniker Dusty (although there was also a Tuffy). Last name Cain—you'll be called "Sugar," as was the case with Matt "Big Sugar" Cain and Bob Cain, the man who pitched to (and naturally walked) the 3'7" Eddie Gaedel, whose strike zone measured a minuscule one-and-a-half inches. It was inevitable that a player named Ivy Andrews be called "Poison," not be confused with the Waner brothers, Paul and Lloyd, aka "Big Poison" and "Little Poison." And Gary Bell answered to the call of "Ding Dong," the same name some announcers called Gus Bell. Meanwhile, a player named George Bell had the occasionally used handle of "Liberty."

Some nicknames were so long, they were impractical. Imagine a PA announcer having to say, "Now hitting, number 37, 'Death to All Flying Things.'" Believe it or not, three men have had that nickname, the most well known probably being Bob Ferguson, who played so long ago (1871–1884) players didn't even wear uniform numbers. He earned his label due to his stellar defensive play; however, he was an infielder but never, as would be expected, an outfielder. According to baseballreference.com, there was a more recent player who had the same nickname, Franklin Gutiérrez (2005–2017), although he never made a big splash in the majors.

Other excessively wordy nicknames include: Frank Chance, "The Peerless Leader"; Pearce Chiles, "What's the Use" (who got that label because when a popup came his way, he'd deride the batter by calling out that catchphrase); Roger Bresnahan, aka "The Duke of Tralee" for his Irish ancestry; and Earl Averill who also had a regal nickname, "The Earl of Snohomish," coming from the name of his hometown.

The unflattering title "Glass Arm Eddie" referred to outfielder Eddie Glass while "Babe Ruth's Legs" was the nickname for Sammy Byrd, who often pinch-ran and became a defensive replacement for an aging Ruth. Rule changes to speed up the game would strip Mike

Hargrove of his nickname had he played nowadays. He was known as "the Human Rain Delay" for his time-consuming gyrations and mannerisms prior to each pitch, not unlike the fidgety Nomar Garciaparra. As former Boston manager Butch Hobson described, "[Hargrove] used to [adjust] his hitting glove, step out of the box, and [fiddle around] with his glove—every pitch."

Some nicknames have a geographic/nationality tie-in: Swede Risberg (one of the eight Black Sox players who threw the 1919 World Series); "The Commerce [Oklahoma] Comet" referred to Mickey Mantle; Bob Feller was sometimes called "Heater From Van Meter [Iowa]"; finally, both Stanley Bordagaray and Jeff Francoeur were commonly called "Frenchy."

Another hand-picked list of some interesting nicknames includes: Max Bishop who was called "Camera Eye"; power hitter Steve "Bye Bye" Balboni; Eric Byrnes's all out style of play gave birth to his alter ego as "Crash Test Dummy"; Marc Rzepczynski (zep-CHIN-skee) was called "Scrabble," and his surname placed on a Scrabble board would rack up plenty of points; along those same lines, Doug Gwosdz (GOO-sh) and Doug Mientkiewicz (mint-KAY-vich) went by "Eye Chart"; Phil "Scrap Iron" Garner; and Yogi Berra's son Dale was sometimes called "Boo Boo" as in Yogi Bear's sidekick.

He wasn't a player, but the son of baseball executive Branch Rickey was a baseball executive. Rickey's offshoot, so to speak, was called "Twig."

Nicknames of some of the all-time greats include: "Double X" (and "Beast") for Jimmie Foxx; Willie Mays was "the Say Hey Kid"; and his slugging teammate was Willie "Stretch" McCovey; "the Splendid Splinter" was Ted Williams; and there is only one "the Man," Stan Musial; however there are two "Hammerin' Hanks"—Aaron and Greenberg; next is "Shoeless Joe" Jackson; Mariano Rivera truly earned the nickname "Sandman"; and no list is complete without Babe Ruth who probably owns the record for the most nicknames including "The Bambino," "The Sultan of Swat," "The Colossus of Clout," and other impractical ones such as "The Behemoth of Bust," and "The Caliph of Clout." Caliph?! Writing styles were certainly different in those days.

Meanwhile, some babies are born with a surname that foreshadowed them being involved with baseball. Johnny Bench seldom sat on the bench, playing in 2,158 games. He was destined to become one of the greatest catchers ever, arguably *the* best.

Others include: Brandon Belt, Darryl Strawberry, Vic Power who had a bit of power (126 homers and 290 doubles), Dave Philley who played three of his 18 seasons with the Phillies, father-son combo Cecil and Prince Fielder, Josh Fields, Ken Singleton who had 1,441 singles among his 2,029 hits, Bruce Hitt who didn't last long (two outings) because he gave up too many of his last names, Coaker Triplett (yes, he hit a few three-base hits—14), Ken and Rich Hill whose combined lifetime win total on the mound exceeded 200, Bob Walk, who gave up 2.7 bases on balls per nine innings, and a whole lot of players named Walker from All-Star brothers Dixie and Harry to Hall of Famer Larry.

Maybe I missed it, but I never heard of a media member doing any wordplay with Al Kaline's name. Type the word alkaline putting a space after the first two letters and you've got the Tigers star's name. So why not a line like, "Kaline has more energy than a truckload of alkaline batteries." You've read worse, right?

Next is a bit of a stretch—Allie Watt and Charlie Watts were both second basemen so they could truly be the ones referred to in the "Who's on first," and "*What's* on second" Abbott and Costello bit.

Finally, a tale of two men with the same surname. During the 10th inning of Game 4 of the 1957 World Series, Milwaukee's Vernal

"Nippy" Jones was sent to the plate as a pinch-hitter. With the Braves down 5–4 to the Yankees, a loss would mean New York just needed one more win to capture the Series.

Jones claimed a low pitch nicked him. Home plate umpire Augie Donatelli said he saw no such thing. Jones produced evidence, showing Donatelli a black smudge on the baseball. Convinced that the mark came from Jones's shoe polish, the ump awarded him first base where he was replaced by a pinch-runner. Soon, that runner scored the tying run and an Eddie Mathews homer gave the Braves a 7–5 comeback win. They went on to top the Yankees in seven games.

Solely because of Jones's unusual encounter, his name remains in baseball history even though that plate appearance, one of just three he'd have in the Series, was the last time he'd appear on a big-league diamond.

Flash forward to the 1969 World Series. As it was being played, there had been a grand total of 12,951 men who had played in the majors. One was Cleon Jones of the Mets. In Game 5 a pitch hit him on the foot, and with the same results—the ump denied Jones a free trip to first base until manager Gil Hodges had him inspect the ball for a shoe polish mark. Jones took first and scored on the next pitch when Donn Clendenon homered, reducing the Orioles lead to 3–2. The Mets went on to win the game, 5–3, and wrap up the World Series.

Now, the probability that over the history of the Series which dates back to 1903, the only two men who were ever involved in a controversial incident involving shoe polish had the same last name, *no matter how common that surname*, is astronomical. Sure, Jones is a common name, but through 1969, only 34 men with that last name had played for any significant amount of time—three or more seasons.

Sidenote: Jones is the third most common last name among major leaguers ever, behind Smith and Johnson and just ahead of Brown and Williams.

Final note: Jerry Koosman was a Mets pitcher in the '69 Series, and he claimed the ball shown to the umpire was doctored, that Hodges instructed him to rub the ball on his shoe.

Chapter 4

Did You See That?! Baseball's Sideshow

Just as carnivals have sideshow attractions which enticed curious customers into shelling out a few dimes to see oddities such as the Fat Woman, the Bearded Woman, and the Sword Swallower, baseball has more than its share of unusual things to behold. So, let's borrow the carnival barker's exhortation: "Hurry! Hurry! Hurry! Step right up to behold baseball's oddities—the freak plays, unbelievable games, and wild events."

There's a quote which basically states a paradox, "If you stick around baseball long enough, you'll see it all—but, you'll also realize that you'll never see everything." Baseball rewards us for our faithful following with displays of some crazy plays and events as it defies another old line stating there's nothing new under the sun (or under the brilliant glare of venues' floodlights).

One tale involves a man who did see something, as they say, with his own eyes, but seeing wasn't believing. In 1902, the Corsicana Oil Citys of the Texas League defeated the Texarkana Casket Makers by the impossible score of 51–3 (you can't make this stuff up). With the concept of a mercy rule decades away, the Oil Citys took no prisoners.

A player named Jay Clarke had a perfect day at the plate—a *really* perfect day as all eight of his hits were homers. Of course, his shots were hardly monumental ones as it is said the right field fence was just

210 feet from home plate in a park not normally used by his team. In fact, his home runs were only a fraction of the 21 his team amassed that day. Corsicana had seven players compile five or more hits. One report said they could have scored even more runs but they became too exhausted. As an added bonus to this sideshow display, the losing pitcher surrendered all 51 runs. The Casket Makers were soon officially pronounced deceased—at the end of the league's first half of the season, the team folded.

The data from the game went out by telegraph to the media. Upon receiving the wire, one operator figured "This can't be right," so he reported the score as 5–3, and credited Clarke with only three home runs, not realizing that just about anything can happen in baseball.

During Game 4 of the 2023 American League Championship Series (ALCS), one of the strangest double plays ever took place. Marcus Semien of the Rangers singled, but was doubled up when Corey Seager scorched a line drive which Houston first baseman Jose Abreu speared. Abreu dove and tagged Semien, able only to graze one finger of Semien's batting glove, which jutted out of his back pocket, for a twin killing the odd way.

Later in that postseason after Semien reached first base, the TV broadcasters made it a point to focus on his gloves, saying they were sure this time the gloves would be well tucked into the depths of his pocket—they were.

The 1954 Cleveland Indians were a team good enough to set a (since broken) AL record by winning 111 games, and their .721 winning percentage is still the all-time league high. It's hard to believe that they could be swept in the World Series, but the Willie Mays led Giants did just that.

And guess what, the team with the loftiest winning percentage ever, the 1906 Cubs, fell in the World Series, too. After winning more than three-fourths of their games (.763), including playing .800 ball on the road, and winning a record 116 games (later tied by the Mariners over a longer season), the Cubs lost the Series in six games to the White Sox.

That Series featured the two teams which, on paper, were further apart talent-wise than any other World Series opponents. That's based on the chasm between their season win totals: The Cubs won 23 more games than the White Sox did.

It's a joy to keep score at the old ballpark or even at home. Why, there's even a book written on the subject. The name? *The Joy of Keeping Score*, of course. Each defensive player is assigned a numeric code. 1 stands for pitchers; 2 = catchers; 3 = first basemen; 4 =second basemen; 5 = third basemen; 6 = shortstops; 7 = left fielders; 8 = center fielders; and 9 represents right fielders.

Gazing over those numbers even years after a game concluded can conjure up images of crisp 3-to-6-to-3 and 3-to-6-to-1 double plays, or the 5-to-4-to-3 around the horn DP. Or how about a rare 6-to-3-to-5 twin killing with an aggressive runner heading for third being gunned down by a slick-fielding first baseman like Keith Hernandez?

Keep score long enough and you'll encounter peculiar plays like a 9-2 putout. In an Orioles game, a slow runner hit a blistering line drive which the right fielder came up with quickly. The first baseman had moved to his right hoping to field the sharply hit ball. The catcher hustled down the line in foul ground in case he had to back up a bad throw from an infielder. Once he saw the ball get through the infield, he wisely covered the first base bag and took the throw from the outfielder to retire the batter.

Then there's the rare 9-3 putout. Right fielders like Roberto Clemente executed such a play at times by defying the axiom about not throwing behind a runner (in this case a runner who had singled then rounded the bag too far).

Another Pirate outfielder, José Guillén, performed a bit of a twist on that play, taking advantage of a slow runner. On May 12, 1998, Pittsburgh was playing the Colorado Rockies when catcher Kirt Manwaring laced a ball sharply into right field for an apparent single. Guillén, however, came up with the ball quickly and rifled it to first base. Embarrassingly, Manwaring was gunned out. Later he likened the experience to the feeling one gets in a dream where you run as hard as you can, but you don't move at all.

That was a great play, but the wildest case of a right fielder getting the ball in to his first baseman came in 1989, when Paul O'Neill was with the Cincinnati Reds. The game was on the line in the ninth inning and the Philadelphia Phillies had Steve Jeltz, representing the potential winning run, in scoring position. A ball was hit into right field where O'Neill, feeling rushed to get off a strong throw to the plate to snuff out the potential game-ending run, bobbled it, juggled it, and then, out of frustration, kicked the ball.

Amazingly, the ball shot directly to Todd Benzinger, his cutoff man at first base. The perplexed baserunner had to hold up at third. Barring such a curious kick, there was no way the Reds could have prevented the winning run from scoring.

Next is the only 7-3 putout in baseball history—it's difficult to conceive a left fielder retiring a batter on a throw to first base! Detroit's Sean Casey was the victim, after hitting what was apparently a clean single on a hard line drive that fell into left field.

Just *how* in the world can that happen? Here's the explanation: Casey's shot first ticked off the glove of a leaping Joe Crede, the White Sox third baseman. Casey, thinking the ball had nestled into Crede's webbing, gave up on the play after taking about three steps down the line. Even though Casey was normally an all-out, hustling guy, he headed back toward his dugout. When he finally realized the ball was alive and in play, he began his dash for first, but it was too late. Pablo Ozuna got to the ball in short left field and rifled a one-bounce throw to first to retire Casey. In truth, since Crede touched the ball, the play is actually scored 5-7-3.

Casey noted, "I've been blessed with a lot of gifts, but speed wasn't one of them. It was a frustrating day for a lot of different reasons, and that was just part of the frustration." Maybe so, but his weird play also makes our list of reasons why we love baseball.

Another puzzler. How do you score the bizarre play in which José Canseco completely misjudged a deep flyball, positively butchered the play—so badly that it hit off his head and bounced over the fence? The temptation is to slap him with a four-base error, but Cleveland batter Carlos Martínez was awarded an unusual home run.

A website called Literary Hub suggests our next homer may be "The Greatest Forgotten Home Run of All Time." If baseball truly had a sideshow, this one would pull in many curious fans. On July 25, 1956, Roberto Clemente got a great Christmas gift five months early. He came to the plate in the bottom of the ninth against the Cubs with the bases loaded—a good spot to be in, but optimism wasn't running high as the Pirates trailed by three runs. Plus, this was not yet the Clemente with a shining résumé. He was only 21, with just one full season behind him, and he had knocked only 10 balls over the fence in his short career.

There is another way of homering, and that's just what he did, drilling a pitch which smacked into a light standard, bounced away, and rolled along the warning track. That gave the three men aboard time to score. Then, despite seeing his third base coach signaling he should hold up at third, Clemente raced through that stop sign, sliding and scoring, just beating a relay throw from Ernie Banks. An inside-the-park, walkoff grand slam. Sheer electricity.

In 1954, Don Larsen led the AL in losses at 3-21, yet the Yankees traded for him in a massive 17-player swap the next season. In 1956, he reached a personal high of just 11 wins, but—and here's the wild part of his story—in that year's World Series this unlikely star added another win to his résumé and became the Series MVP. How? By throwing the only postseason perfect game ever. That led to a famous quote calling the hard-drinking Larsen "the imperfect man who pitched a perfect game." A not-too-bright reporter asked Larsen, "Is this the best game you ever pitched?"

Baseball has even given us crazy happenings such as the time a game in Baltimore was witnessed by absolutely zero fans. On April 29, 2015, the Orioles hosted a game 10 days after an African American was seriously injured while in police custody, setting off protests. That led to enough unrest that the previous two games had been postponed. Lacking enough security workers for the game, the decision was made to play the game in front of an empty house, a first.

Maybe it wasn't exactly a funhouse attraction, but those who heard about what happened in Boston when Braves Field held its 1946 Opening Day initially may have been amused at the folly of it all. The park had gone through a new paint job, but nobody factored in the damp and cold Boston weather. Before too long hundreds of fans discovered they had sat on wet paint. The club had to pick up hefty cleaning bills and dish out money for the apologetic ad they placed in the newspaper.

Dodgers officials were all set to unveil their new jewel when it was discovered that despite all the effort put into the planning and construction of Ebbets Field, the key to the main gate, the key to the bleachers, and the American flag had all been forgotten. That was bad enough, but the architect had also neglected to include a press box in his plans (the park had no press box until 1929).

At least those issues didn't stop the game, but the home opener of the 1907 New York Giants was interrupted when their failure to get rid of all the snow that had hit the city led to a problem. With the Giants trailing badly in the game, fans took up another diversion, pitching snowballs onto the field. The umpires wound up halting the game.

Adrián Beltré got in trouble for moving the on-deck circle. No, this was no strong man act, the circle was simply a plastic mat players are expected to stand on while waiting for their turn at bat. Late in a game when his Rangers were losing, 18–6, he was standing several feet away from the circle, not on it. An ump instructed him to get on the mat. Beltré simply lifted the mat and pulled it over to the area where he wanted to stand. He explained he was less likely to get hit by a foul ball there—no disrespect intended. Nevertheless, he was ejected from the game for what was perceived as an act of defiant showmanship, even though he could certainly argue he *was* standing in the on-deck circle, albeit in a new location.

Babe Ruth did some incredible things on diamonds beyond his home-run feats. For instance, thanks to the exploits of Shohei Ohtani, Ruth's name has come up frequently of late for his pitching prowess. Ruth once led the AL in ERA at 1.75 and once held the record for the most consecutive shutout innings in World Series play. Perhaps more surprising is that he stole home 10 times in his career. His hitting a career high of 16 triples in 1921 is also hard to believe.

Before discussing Ruth's rambling adventures on the basepaths, some background on one of baseball's most exciting and daring plays. Lou Brock once held the stolen base record for a season (118) and career (938). The man who broke Brock's records (with 130 and 1,406), the mercurial Rickey Henderson, only managed to steal home four times. The tactic was much more common long ago, with Ty Cobb listed as having 32 swipes of home to his credit, including six in one season. An article written by Bill Nowlin for the Society of American Baseball Research stated, "A player has stolen home twice in the same game a reported 11 times."

Cobb even stole his way around the bases three times. On one of those occasions, he stole second, third, then home on three straight pitches! And, three times he was the lead runner, stealing home on triple steals.

Now, one of the main reasons old-timers tried this ploy much more often than current players is the more lively ball—today's players don't need to scrape for runs when they can rip the ball for more long hits than before. Don't forget, many of the old-timers' steals of home came on the back end of double steals.

As for Ruth, most of his steals of home came that way. Nevertheless, he did pilfer 123 bases lifetime, and *that* defies the image some fans have of a beer-bellied, lead-footed player who was better suited for softball fields than for Cooperstown fame.

In the third game of the 1921 World Series he must have delighted and dazzled fans when he stole second then proceeded to burgle the next base, too. In addition to that, in 1918, his theft of home accounted for the winning run in a game in which he got the victory with a 3–1, complete-game outing. That World Series also marked the last time a starting pitcher was penciled into a lineup slot other than ninth. He batted sixth and came through with a triple, driving home two runs in a 3–2 Red Sox win.

Ruth was a sensational one-man sideshow, a freak of nature. Discounting the men whose names have been tainted by suspicion and/or actual guilt of using performance-enhancing drugs (PEDs), Ruth, seemingly fueled on beer and hot dogs, still ranks number one for career WAR (Wins Above Replacement). He's also second in home runs only to Hank Aaron, he's ranked number 2 with his ratio of one home run per every 11.76 at-bats, and he's tied for third place on the lifetime runs scored list.

Even counting every man who ever played baseball, he's first in both slugging percentage and on-base plus slugging, second for the highest on-base percentage, trailing only Ted Williams, and third for runs driven in, averaging just a bit over 100 per season. One other stat few people today are aware of is that his lifetime batting average of .342 ranked number five among modern-era players upon his retirement.

His legacy and dominance were molded of cement, so much so that when he died in 1948, it had been 29 years since his last season of pitching for the Red Sox, yet he still owned the highest winning percentage of any other pitcher going up *against the Yankees*. After Boston sold him to the Yankees, he hit more home runs than the entire Red Sox squad in 10 of the following dozen seasons.

In 1920, when he hit 54 homers, 14.6 percent of all AL homers came off his bat. His total set a new season record, and almost doubled the 29 homers he had hit the previous season when he first took over the all-time single-season record. Over his 22-year career, he led the league in homers 12 times, and was the AL runner-up three more times.

Trivia note: Ruth, who earned an estimated $856,850 for his entire big-league career, hit only one homer in the minors—and that one came on foreign soil. That shot came in Toronto, then in the International League, when Ruth, who tossed a shutout that day, was only 19.

Surprisingly, and despite a great line written about Ruth, "The Babe is mighty and shall prevail"—a twist of the famous line, "Truth is mighty and will prevail"—the truth is he didn't *always* succeed. And that leads to a Ripley-like story about a pitcher who, in old baseball slang, "owned" Babe Ruth, thwarting him time and time again.

At just 5'10", Hub "Shucks" Pruett was the man with this Ruthian jinx. He got his nickname because uttering the word "shucks" was the closest he ever got to swearing. His main motivation for playing pro ball was to earn enough money to pay for medical school. Playing ball, it took him eight years to get his degree, but after attending six schools including Harvard, he did become a physician.

The southpaw pitcher had a secret weapon, one which "befuddled the Babe," his fadeaway pitch, what we'd now call a screwball. Reporters called it "The pitch that bamboozled Babe."

A story from the *Louisville Courier Journal* by Tommy Fitzgerald quoted Pruett's catcher, Hank Severeid, as saying, "Pruett had the greatest fadeaway I've ever seen. Carl Hubbell was given a lot of credit for the one he had, but compared with Pruett's, it was like a single shingle nail compared to a 20-penny spike." He also said of Pruett's usual strategy, "He had thrown Ruth nothing but the fadeaway all season. He was death on left-handed hitters like Ruth."

However, that strategy changed one day when the catcher got inspired to call for a fastball. It would be the only time Pruett gave him a fastball. Ruth, not baffled this time, homered, elated to have his diet of fadeaways temporarily come to an end. Pruett later pointed out that when Ruth homered, the ball left the playing field right where the park would later have a screen. That meant Ruth's blast would have gone for a double, leaving him homerless versus Pruett (but one source has Ruth hitting two total homers off his nemesis). The pitcher later stated, "Seeing the Babe strike out was almost as exciting as seeing him hit a home run."

Hub Pruett, the man who "owned" Babe Ruth. The slugger who hit .342 lifetime was befuddled by Pruett, hitting just .167 one season versus the pitcher. COURTESY OF THE LIBRARY OF CONGRESS

Now, Ruth wound up being a lifetime .342 hitter, but he experienced futility versus Pruett: seven hits in 28 at-bats for a relatively paltry batting average of .250. And, if Pruett found it exciting to watch Ruth strike out, he certainly got his fill of that as he fanned the Babe 14 times, in 56 percent of Ruth's at-bats against him (at-bats, *not* plate appearances—to be fair Ruth did draw seven walks).

As a mere rookie, Pruett whiffed Ruth nine times over the slugger's first official 10 at-bats, and in his other at-bat Babe grounded out to Pruett. Ruth did coax three walks in between, though. The star who would hit .322 on the year could only muster a .167 batting average against Pruett.

Once against Pruett, Ruth even laid down a sacrifice bunt, hardly a Ruthian move. The pitcher's rookie season ended with a 7-7 record, an ERA of 2.33, 70 total strikeouts, and a league-leading 23 games finished. Perhaps overworked as a rookie, Pruett said, "I was a mediocre pitcher after 1923." Tell that to Ruth!

Over Pruett's three AL seasons, Ruth batted against him in 14 games, and he struck out in nine of those games. In games when Pruett pitched at least twice to Ruth, there was only one occasion when he didn't put him down at least once on strikes. In the five games in which Ruth batted four or five times versus Pruett, he went down on strikes three times in two of those contests and twice on one other occasion. No wonder Ruth called him his biggest jinx.

Pruett looked back on his initial encounter with the Babe. "It didn't bother me, facing Ruth for the first time [in 1922]. When I went out to the mound, I didn't know who he was. I struck him out on three pitches. All I knew was he batted left-handed and I didn't have much trouble with left-handers."

Pruett once mused, "What got me a reputation in baseball and kept me in baseball were those dramatic strikeouts of Ruth."

Pruett also said that when they were active players, they would "pass each other without ever speaking. But every once in a while Ruth did something that gave me a kick. He would wink at me."

Their first conversation was many years later, in 1948, about two months before Ruth died. They were at a baseball dinner in St. Louis. Pruett said, "I went up and introduced myself and said, 'Thanks, Babe, for putting me through medical school. If it hadn't been for you, nobody would have ever heard of me.' Babe Ruth remembered me. He said, 'That's all right, kid, but I'm glad there weren't many more like you or no one would have heard of me.'"

The first time Pruett faced another pretty good left-handed hitter, Ty Cobb, he inherited a 3-0 count. "I got Cobb on three straight strikes [all fadeaways]." Saving face, and a dour one at that, Cobb muttered, "That kid won't last long with that crazy pitch." Pruett had the last word, "He was wrong because I pitched for seven years."

Pruett did stick around, but his hex over Ruth wasn't indicative of his overall performance—he went 29-48 with a lofty ERA of 4.63. So, the man who "owned" Ruth ironically struggled against most other batters.

While Aroldis Chapman is credited with throwing the fastest pitch ever at 105.8 mph, another diamond king deserves recognition. Fans were astonished at the performances of the King and His Court, an unbeatable four-man (pitcher, catcher, shortstop, and first baseman) softball team featuring Eddie Feigner with his ever-present crewcut for a crown. He topped out with a scorching 112 mph pitch according to an ESPN story by Jim Caple.

Feigner, who said he could win with just himself and his catcher, once struck out a batter while hurling from center field. As if bored with the normal way to pitch, he'd put on a show, at times throwing almost effortlessly from behind his back or from between his legs. He even pitched when blindfolded.

Checking out some of his videos on YouTube is highly recommended. Beyond his astounding pitching, he and his team put on an eye-popping show. After receiving a return throw from his catcher, Feigner immediately whipped the ball behind his back, picking off a runner from second. Another time his court pulled off a double steal—the runner from first took off for second, and at the same time, a runner from second took off to "steal" first base. The team's Globetrotter-like exhibitions entertained a legion of fans from coast to coast and beyond, in a reported 100 countries.

From the late 1940s into the 2000 season, he won 9,743 games while racking up 141,516 strikeouts, 930 no-hitters, and 238 perfect games. He faced great hitters, too. In a 1967 softball exhibition contest, throwing from the regulation 45 feet from the plate, he K'ed Willie Mays, Willie McCovey, Brooks Robinson, Harmon Killebrew, Roberto Clemente, and Maury Wills *in a row*. He barnstormed endlessly, traveling "to towns even McDonald's ignores."

Then there's the legendary minor-league pitcher named Steve Dalkowski who some say could throw a baseball 110+ mph despite his 5'11" and 170-pound frame. He was so wild, though, in one game he struck out 24 hapless batters, but permitted 18 men to reach base. He threw in six wild pitches for bad measure. Overall, in his first season out of high school in the Appalachian League he threw 62 innings, fanned 121, but walked 129 men. It's been written that his career was, at least in part, the inspiration for the *Bull Durham* character Nuke LaLoosh.

Some stories about his speed may be apocryphal, yet fascinating. A few include a tale that one of his pitches ripped a batter's earlobe off. His pitches were so forceful they broke wooden planks and wiring on backstops. Ted Williams faced him and called him the fastest pitcher he ever saw.

Another man who had trouble locating the strike zone was Ryne Duren. Older fans still remember him peering through the thick Coke-bottle lenses of his glasses to pick up his catcher's sign, then unleashing a pitch high up on the netting behind the plate. His vision was 20/70 in one eye and 20/200 in the other eye. Finding the plate was a constant task for Duren.

Still, he turned his handicap into an advantage—they say when he entered a game his first warmup pitch was intentionally uncorked with the purpose of pelting the screen behind the plate to get into batters' minds. It didn't help hitters who were aware he once said he never pitched an inning in his career when he was sober. Another time he knocked down Jimmy Piersall—when he was *standing in the on-deck circle.*

Nolan Ryan walked more batters than any other major leaguer, but his overall overpowering ways paved his way to Cooperstown. One of his catchers was Jeff Torborg, who said, "Nolan threw it down the strike zone harder than any human being I ever saw. In 1973, against the Boston Red Sox, Nolan threw a pitch a little up and over my left shoulder. I reached up for it and his pitch tore a hole in the webbing of my glove and hit the backstop."

Speaking of speed, it's actually humorous to learn how early fastball artists were so primitively clocked. In response to curiosity about just how fast a Bob Feller fastball flew, a laughable way to measure it was devised.

A motorcycle traveling at 86 mph sped by Feller who threw the ball at a paper target 60'6" away. It turned out the cycle was 10 feet ahead of Feller when he let go of the baseball, but the ball hit the bull's-eye about three feet before the motorcycle reached that location.

The experimenters' unscientific conclusion was the pitch topped 100 mph (107.6, unofficially). It should be noted that Feller was throwing off a flat surface, not a raised mound, and did so wearing dress slacks and a shirt with a necktie to boot. No joke—this is also on YouTube.

Another time a somewhat more sophisticated method was used by the US Army to clock Feller. Their measuring device, which used photoelectric cells, was originally made to measure the speed of shells used in World War II. This test yielded a result that Feller had set a new speed record at 98.6 mph.

Fans have always gotten into it when managers and umpires *really* got into it. With the use of replays to resolve close calls, showstopping confrontations between the men in blue and larger-than-life managers such as Leo Durocher, a notorious umpire baiter, now occur less often.

Hall of Fame umpire Jocko Conlan once went toe-to-toe with Durocher, a man who truly deserved his nickname "Leo the Lip." Durocher got on Conlan from the bench, but when things escalated, he bolted from the dugout charging directly at Conlan. The two men argued back and forth over a call at the plate, seemingly ready to engage in hand-to-hand combat. Instead, it turned out to be more a case of a foot-to-foot battle.

Here's how that played out: On April 16, 1961, after their verbal altercation raged on for some time, Durocher escalated things. He claimed he tried to kick dirt on Conlan's trousers, but connected instead to a leg. The umpire was unintimidated by the bully tactics and kicked right back. Durocher wasn't one to take that, so he kicked once more. Undaunted, Conlan returned fire. Finally it dawned on Durocher that the ump had a few secret allies. This fight card was over—Conlan won in sort of a TKO.

In an article Durocher and Ed Linn wrote for the *Saturday Evening Post*, Leo explained why he threw in the towel. Umpires, he noted, wore iron plates attached to their shoes' toes. Every Conlan kick resulted in a lump to Durocher's shins, but the kicks from The lip to Conlan's shin guards were harmless, except to Leo's toes. One writer said the two men first went chin-to-chin then shin-to-shin.

Conlan's account of the incident is that Durocher called him "a dumb Irishman . . . I don't know who's dumb, but I had shin guards on and he didn't. I left him limping for two weeks with bruises as big as silver dollars."

Fans love colorful characters and those who hunger to win. Well, Durocher was famous for his fiery will to win. To emphasize that drive, he once said that if he was playing third base and his mother was rounding the bag on her way to score the winning run he would trip her. "I'd pick her up and brush her off, and then I'd say, 'Sorry, Mom, but nobody beats me.'"

When his mother heard what he had said, she was hurt and indignant. "You said that about your own mother? You'd trip me, son, your own mother?" He tried to placate her saying his comments were merely exaggerations, but knowing him she was still left in disbelief.

Author Jonathan Eig wrote, "If Durocher spoke a sentence without curses, it was probably an accident, soon to be corrected." And Branch Rickey once called the colorful Durocher "a man with an infinite capacity for making a bad situation immediately worse."

In fact, another writer, Jim Murray, wrote that Durocher had the ability to take a third-place team and finish first with it, but that he was also capable of taking a 10th-place team and finishing 11th, which, of course was impossible in a 10-team league.

Earl Weaver was also a master of confrontation. He got right in an umpire's face, then animatedly bobbed his head as he vociferously made his case. As his head moved, he was "accidentally" pecking the ump with the peak of his cap. He is said to have purposely spewed out words, like those starting with the letter P, which resulted in him "unintentionally" spitting his venom in a spray toward umpires.

Weaver showed up umpires by carrying a rulebook onto the field to cite rules which proved his point. He once buried the book near home plate as if to say, "If you won't enforce the rules, let's just pronounce this book to be dead." When an ump instructed him not to display the rulebook, Weaver's retort was, "There ain't no rule in the rulebook about bringing a rulebook on the field." Like a precocious child, he always tried to get the last word in.

Some managers are colorful for other types of actions. Managers who get kicked out of games have been known to hide from the view of umpires by going down some dugout steps. Bobby Valentine did something no other manager has done before or since. After getting the thumb, he left the dugout only to return to the bench shortly after wearing an absurd disguise. It consisted of sunglasses (during a night game) and two pieces of eye-black tape stuck on his upper lip to resemble a cheesy mustache. The MLB website stated the tape gave "him a Hercule Poirot-style mustache." He almost looked like he was wearing the novelty glasses that come with fake eyebrows, large nose, and mustache—giving him a sort of Groucho Marx look, too.

Hardly an act of going incognito, he was soon caught by TV cameras, re-ejected by the umpires, and later suspended for two games and fined $5,000.

A minor-league manager once outdid Valentine. After he got the thumb, he commandeered the birdlike costume from his team's mascot before returning to the game. At one point he wanted to make a strategic move, but to do so, he had to get the attention of the acting manager without revealing his identity to everyone. He approached the man and mumbled something like, "Change pitchers—bring Smith in." The acting skipper had to be thinking, "Who does this guy think he is? I don't take orders from a mascot." Finally, to get his order across, the real manager had to pry the bird's beak apart, opening it wide enough to reveal his face. This time the message he chirped out was obeyed.

Chapter 5

More of the Unusual and Odd

Another strength of baseball is the fact that no matter how long the game has been around, there's always somebody who comes along to shatter a revered record or achieve something that's never been done before—sometimes it's something awesome, other times it may just be something unusual. Further, frequently watching games gives fans the opportunity to perhaps witness some such occurrence, and when that does take place, what a thrill it provides.

Baseball records should not be carved in stone—writing them on an Etch A Sketch toy or a dry-erase board might make more sense, because as sure as a record is deemed to be unbreakable, someone comes along to erase it.

Start with events from 2023, with Ronald Acuña Jr.'s amazing performance when he became baseball's first ever 40/70 man with his 41 homers and 73 stolen bases. At one time, the 30-30 Club seemed to be ritzy, exclusive—after Ken Williams became the charter member in 1922, nobody else joined him until 1956 (Willie Mays), and through 1969 only four men had reached those levels in a single season.

Since then, there have been multiple seasons when four men have joined the group. Not only that, until 1987, a player came up with those numbers only 11 times. Now, that group has swollen, and the feat has been done 68 times through 2023, with quite a few of the power and speed guys turning in multiple seasons of 30 or more slugs and steals.

During the wild card round in the 2023 postseason, Philadelphia's Craig Kimbrel did something which is believed to be a playoff first. With Miami's Josh Bell on second base after his leadoff double, and Bryan De La Cruz at the plate in the ninth inning of the Phillies' series-clinching contest, Kimbrel enjoyed a three-run lead. He had already retired two men after the Bell double, but he took nothing for granted. What did he do? He dropped the baseball as he stood on the rubber, resulting in a balk. The odd part? He did that intentionally. Worried that Bell might gaze in and steal his signs then relay them to De La Cruz, Kimbrel willingly let Bell, who represented a meaningless run, advance one base. Moments later, he induced De La Cruz to ground out and the Phillies advanced.

While this made some highlight reels, it's been said that the first pitcher to intentionally balk runners over to third base was Bob Wickman in 2005, and he did this more than once. He felt more comfortable with the runner over one notch instead of behind him at second base. Another pitcher known to have done this was Kenley Jansen.

Another event from the 2023 postseason was unexpected. Sure, Clayton Kershaw had suffered through some extremely shaky playoff outings, but his first start in the NL Division Series was a shocker. The sure thing Hall of Famer, winner of three Cy Young Awards, an MVP trophy, five ERA crowns, and a pitcher's Triple Crown in 2011, lasted a mere one-third of an inning against Arizona. He left the game having faced eight batters and after having been battered for six hits and six earned runs, which amounted to a miserable ERA of 162.0!

To put this in perspective, through 16 seasons and 425 games his ERA stood at 2.48, and in 2023, he posted a slightly better ERA of

2.46 as if to show he wasn't slowing down. But his disastrous playoff performance took his lifetime postseason ERA up to 4.49, more than two points worse than his regular-season numbers. His overall playoff stats, covering his first 39 appearances, paints an indelible stain on his otherwise standout career.

Yet another oddity that occurred in 2023 was one that really wasn't new, but it came across as a throwback to the daring days of Ty Cobb. After Elly De La Cruz singled, he swiped second, and shortly after took third without a throw being made. The pitcher, Milwaukee's Elvis Peguero, was visibly flustered. He took the return toss from his catcher and trudged back to the mound. Seeing the pitcher's leisurely, contemplative walk, De La Cruz began to stroll down the third base line. When Peguero still paid no mind to De La Cruz, it was time to take off for home. A hurried throw home was too late.

The last big leaguer to take such a trek around the bases was Miami's Jon Berti in 2020, but De La Cruz made it special in that he took his tour on only *two pitches*. As a matter of fact, he was the first player to steal three bases in a single plate appearance since Rod Carew in 1961. This rare crowd-pleasing feat will always remain an electrifying one for baseball fans.

If you had to guess what was the most recent season in which a Cleveland team's combined home-run total for its outfielders was just 18, what would you guess? A student of baseball history would logically first consider the Dead Ball Era, but this happened in 2023 when the Guardians' usual center fielder, Myles Straw hit just one homer. Why, Albert Belle could hit 18 in one month—well, almost. In 1995, he did hit 17 in September alone.

One final event from 2023 was so different, it had never before been accomplished: Miami's Luis Arráez won the National League batting title, matching the title he had won in 2022 for the Twins. He is the first player to win back-to-back batting crowns while playing not only for two different teams, but in two different major leagues.

In 2020, D. J. LeMahieu had become the first modern day player to win a title in both leagues. He won his AL crown while with the Yankees four years after capturing a title as a member of the Rockies.

In a related oddity, Willie McGee was traded in July of 1990 even though at the time of the deal he was leading the NL in hitting at .335. However, his Cardinals team was a cellar dweller and McGee was eligible to become a free agent the next year. At season's end when he had officially won the NL title, he was wearing the jersey of the Oakland Athletics. That made him the first player ever to win the crown in one league while finishing the season in a different league. The ruling was that at the time he was sent packing he already had enough plate appearances to qualify for the batting title.

Interestingly, he only hit .274 with the A's, meaning his overall batting average on the season was .324, which wasn't even high enough to finish in the top five for the entire majors—Eddie Murray's .330 for the Dodgers was the best in the majors, yet he lost the NL crown to McGee. Plus, McGee did collect a major-league-leading 199 hits, but he didn't lead *either league* in that department.

Even the all-time greats have had times when their manager pinch-hit for them. The player who went to the plate for such stars could brag, for instance, "I once replaced Ted Williams." What was so strange about the man who did hit for Williams in 1960 is that he, Carroll Hardy, was a lifetime .225 hitter while Williams hit .344 for his career. There's more: Less than a year after filling in for "The Splendid Splinter," Hardy pinch-hit for a Red Sox rookie who was Cooperstown bound, Carl Yastrzemski.

Also noteworthy is the fact that Williams had close to 10,000 plate appearances and was only pinch-hit for once—and that was only because during an at-bat he painfully fouled a ball off his foot and had to limp off the field. Hardy, unlike the fictional Joe Hardy who helped defeat the Yankees in a famous movie, hit into a double play. When Williams homered in his final at-bat, it was Hardy who once more took Williams's place, this time as a defensive replacement.

Hardy was a trivia lover's delight for other reasons—on his birthday in 1958, he also pinch-hit for Roger Maris, and in that at-bat he homered. One more thing: He played one season in the NFL and caught a touchdown pass from another Hall of Famer, Y. A. Tittle.

Ty Cobb was number one for lifetime hits, 4,189, for many years, yet a player who wound up with 194 career hits once pinch-hit for Cobb. Fred Payne ended his career with a .215 batting average, but he could honestly say he replaced a .366 hitter in a game.

One other Yaz item of interest. Neal Heaton faced Carl Yastrzemski when Heaton was a rookie in 1982, and Yaz was 42 years old, one season away from retirement. The previous year, Heaton, then in college, pitched against Yastrzemski's son, Mike. But, no, Heaton never faced the grandson of Yaz, also named Mike and now in the majors.

In 1988, when the Yankees held an Old-Timers' Game, they brought back members of their 1978 squad. On that day, the active roster of the Yankees listed a 45-year-old pitcher, the ageless Tommy John, who was older than every one of the old-timers.

In a similar tale of an old pitcher, when the 1982 season began, baseball graybeard Gaylord Perry, then 43, had more lifetime wins (297) than his Mariners franchise owned in their history (290).

When Maury Wills stole 104 bases to break Cobb's single-season record, he virtually came out of nowhere. Well, not quite—he had led the NL in steals the previous two seasons, his first full ones in the majors, but with totals of only 50 and 35. His one-year improvement of 69 steals qualified as an oddity, yet another one that baseball lovers relish.

Juan Marichal was a baseball victim of circumstance in the 1960s. He was among the top 10 NL pitchers in ERA seven seasons, and in the top five for wins six times—in fact, his 191 victories topped every other pitcher. But, he went through the entire decade and not only never won the Cy Young Award, he *never got a single vote* for that honor. The only time he cracked the top 10 was in 1971, the season he came in eighth in the voting.

Until 1967, only one award was given out for the majors, not one trophy winner from each league. Also, winning the award wasn't easy when one went up against the likes of Sandy Koufax, Bob Gibson, and Don Drysdale—but still, not one vote?!

Of course, Ted Williams won the Triple Crown in 1942 and 1947 and hit .406 in 1941, and all he had to show for it MVP-wise was three second-place finishes (although he did win that honor two times in all).

In 1935, slugger Hank Greenberg had already reached the 100 RBI mark by, get this, the All-Star break. He had accumulated an incredible 103 RBIs (of the 170 he'd end up with), and he did that in just 76 games, which is less than half of a season—they played 154-game schedules back then. He also had 25 homers by the break, a .317 batting average, and an on-base plus slugging percentage (OPS) of 1.062.

Despite being on a tear by the break, the 24-year-old Greenberg was *not* on that year's All-Star squad. Back then he was playing first base, not the outfield as would later be the case, and two other first basemen were chosen instead of Greenberg despite his awesome production and, unforgivably, even though his own manager selected the All-Star squad!

The two first basemen weren't too shabby: Lou Gehrig, who played the entire game at first, and Jimmie Foxx, who played almost the whole game, but did so out of position as the starting third baseman.

The Cincinnati Reds once fielded a team which featured two sets of brothers handling all four of the infield positions. The Boone brothers, Aaron and Bret, were playing third and second respectively. Barry Larkin was at his normal spot at shortstop while his brother Stephan, playing in his only big-league game ever, was stationed at first base to round out this specially arranged event, held on the final day of the 1988 season.

The Reds had also played a game two years earlier which featured six players in their lineup who were native Cincinnatians. It took place on August 17, 1986, and it marked the last time Pete Rose, then the team's player/manager, ever played in the majors. The others were starting pitcher Chris Welsh out of Xavier High School in Cincinnati, shortstop Larkin, Buddy Bell at third, Ron Oester at second base, and Dave Parker in right field.

In 1969, the Cubs pulled off a rarity when, excluding outfielders and pitchers, all of their other starters were named to the All-Star Game roster: Ernie Banks at first; Glenn Beckert at second; shortstop Don Kessinger; Ron Santo at third; and Randy Hundley behind the plate.

The 1963 Cardinals entire infield started that year's All-Star Game with Bill White stationed at first base; Dick Groat at short; Ken Boyer at the hot corner; and Julian Javier playing second after the man voted in to start the contest, Bill Mazeroski, had to bow out due to an injury.

Roger Craig's career featured a big coincidental event. He was the starting pitcher in both the last game ever played by his Brooklyn Dodgers and the first starter to take the mound for the New York Mets. That season fans began to fall in love with the hapless Mets, finding their ineptitude refreshing when contrasted with the Yankees and their corporate image.

The 1962 Mets defied the adage that every big-league team is inevitably going to win one-third of their games and lose one-third (with the results in the other third determining a team's fate). No, they couldn't win 33.3 percent of their games; they went 40-120, winning just 25 percent of their contests.

Craig was good enough to lead his club in wins. Unfortunately, his 10 wins (25 percent of the team's victories) were offset by 24 losses. The team had two 20-game losers and another who lost 19. Yet another, who worked 36 games out of the bullpen, somehow managed to lose 17 games (3-17 overall). Finally, another starter went 1-12. Clearly, this is one team that didn't get calluses from celebratory handshakes.

The box score of one of the most unusual games ever featured perfect symmetry. In August of 1910, the Pirates and Dodgers played to an 8–8 tie with both teams having exactly 38 at-bats, 13 hits, 12 assists, two errors, five strikeouts, three walks, one hit batsman, and one passed ball, defying all odds.

Wes Ferrell was pitching for the Red Sox on August 22, 1934, and was trailing, 2–1, in the eighth inning. He changed that in a hurry with a solo homer. Still tied in the 10th inning, Ferrell batted again with two men out. He did it again. His second home run of the day was a walkoff. Ferrell still holds the record for the most career homers hit by a pitcher, a staggering 38, and he hit .280 lifetime with a season high of .364.

If you were in the stands on that same date in 1971, you would have seen a game which started *and* concluded with a solo home run for the winning Athletics. And, those homers provided the only runs for Oakland that day. Bert Campaneris led off with his home run, and in the last of the ninth Reggie Jackson won it with more of a run-off home run than a walkoff, climaxing the game with an inside-the-park homer.

A big-league pitcher once got three outs on one pitch. Cincinnati's Ken Ash was called into a game in 1930 with two men on and nobody out. Chicago's Charlie Grimm promptly hit into a triple play. Ash was lifted for a pinch-hitter and the Reds scored the go-ahead run, so on one pitch he got credit for a full inning of work and a win.

What other sport has featured such unique trades as a broadcaster for a player? Ernie Harwell was in the booth for the Atlanta Crackers in 1948, and was doing such a fine job that part owner of the Dodgers, Branch Rickey, wanted him to fill in for an ailing Red Barber. The Crackers were willing to surrender the future Hall of Fame broadcaster, but only in exchange for a player. That deal sent catcher Cliff Dapper to Atlanta in the only such trade in baseball history. Of course in another unprecedented move, the Astros once got rid of a manager and replaced him with Larry Dierker, who had been working as one of their announcers.

The Tigers and Indians once pulled off an odd trade, exchanging managers, with Joe Gordon going to Detroit and Jimmy Dykes switching to Cleveland. Both teams finished below .500.

In late 1976, the Pirates coveted Athletics manager Chuck Tanner and were willing to ship a player, Manny Sanguillén (plus $100,000) to Pittsburgh to get Tanner under contract. In his third year at the helm of the Pirates, Tanner steered them to the world championship. Interestingly, Sanguillén spent just one year in Oakland before being traded back to the Pirates.

And a Bleacher Report story tells of one player, Tim Fortugno, who was dealt from his Reno Silver Sox team in exchange for a bucket of baseballs. Well, the whole story is the Brewers organization wanted to buy Fortugno, but their offer of $2,500 wasn't good enough. The deal was finally sealed when the Brewers agreed to toss in 12 dozen baseballs.

Incidentally, there have been a few other players involved in a trade which featured equipment, and even one involving oysters (but that tale is for another day).

In a bizarre swap, two players were traded between games of a doubleheader with both winding up playing for two teams on the same day. On Memorial Day in 1922, the Cubs were hosting the Cardinals in a twinbill. They agreed to make a trade which sent Max Flack to the Cards in exchange for Cliff Heathcote, and both men saw action in both ends of the doubleheader. So, in the nightcap, the men were both trying to help the team to victory that they had earlier been trying to knock off.

That unique deal calls to mind the time Joel Youngblood was traded and wound up playing for two teams in two different cities on the same day. He even ended the day by collecting a hit for both clubs, *and against two future Hall of Famers*!

On August 4, 1982, Youngblood began the day as the starting center fielder for the Mets, and he went 1-for-2 in a matinee game at Wrigley Field. After playing for several innings, and not long after singling in two runs against Fergie Jenkins, he was informed that he had been traded to the Expos, who wanted him to report right away.

He hurriedly gathered up his gear and belongings and flew to Philadelphia. There, in the sixth inning, he was inserted into the game as a pinch-hitter. Facing Steve Carlton, Youngblood reached on an infield single and played the rest of the game. Not a bad day's work.

As the owner of the Athletics, some of Charlie Finley's antics got him into trouble with the league office. For instance, he felt the New York Yankees home park's short right field fence gave them an unfair advantage, what with their many left-handed pull hitters from

Babe Ruth to Roger Maris. The short distance directly down the right field line at Yankee Stadium—which was grandfathered in after a new rule dictated a minimum distance to any park's fence—meant a poke of 296 feet could result in a home run. A similar drive in Finley's Municipal Stadium in Kansas City might be nothing more than a routine out.

Seeking justice, equity, and an edge for his team, he altered his ballpark, adding a new section of seats in 1964 which he called the "K-C Pennant Porch." This involved creating a fence that curved from right-center field until it met a shorter, straight section of fence, at the 296 feet marker. The shorter fence angled out sharply and directly (*and crazily*) from the foul pole. In other words, while the foul pole was, at 325 feet, a decent distance from the plate, the straight fence ran almost right on top of the foul line—a fair ball hit into the tiny corner between that fence and the line provided virtually no room for an outfielder to venture (and he'd have to hook himself around the fence's sharp angle in order to reach such a ball). The space between the foul line and the fence ranged between a centimeter in width to, at the very most, five feet, and it resembled an acute angle seen nowhere outside of a geometry class.

So, while the distance from the batter to the location where the foul line met the pole may have been legal, much of his "porch," in home-run territory, was a shorter, rather ludicrous drive—just what Finley wanted. A sketch of the right field territory would resemble the scribbling of a child done under the influence of hiccups. Needless to say, Finley had to dismantle this monstrosity. After just two exhibition games he was ordered by baseball commissioner Ford Frick to, in the parlance of the theater, "strike the set."

Unruffled, Finley ordered a "One-Half Pennant Porch" be constructed. This one did feature a proper distance of 325 feet in right

Venerable Yankee Stadium in its opening season, 1923. Its appropriate nickname was "The House That Ruth Built." COURTESY OF THE LIBRARY OF CONGRESS

field. It was permitted to stay, but it didn't help. The Athletics lost 105 games.

Sidenote: Speaking of making the hitting of home runs easier as Finley tried to do, some ballparks, such as the cookie-cutter venues, did the opposite, having high walls making home-run hitting more difficult, *and* the crowd-pleasing robbing of homers nearly impossible. Many neoclassical parks such as PNC Park purposely installed shorter fences, something really classic parks such as Yankee Stadium and Dodger Stadium seemingly had forever.

A language purist can take joy in baseball's colorful lingo and even take a bit of a perverse pleasure in correcting blunders. Many announcers have been guilty of using redundancies, the unnecessary use of more than one word or phrase which means the same thing.

One example: Some ads state, "Order now and get a bonus—a *free gift*." That's clearly redundant—if you get a gift, it *is* free. Nobody gives you a Christmas gift then says, "Oh, by the way, you owe me $19.99." Three fairly common baseball examples of redundancies: "It's a full count of 3-and-2," and "It's a scoreless tie," and "He hit a grand slam home run."

Baseball's unpredictability, another charm of the game, is often intriguing and puzzling. How can a pitcher go from a 2-0 record with a 1.00 ERA in the 1971 World Series to not even being able to locate home plate two seasons later? Pittsburgh's Steve Blass did just that. A 19-game winner in 1972, he not just misplaced, but *totally and irretrievably* lost his baseball radar—becoming incapable of throwing strikes. In 1973, he tumbled to a 3-9 record and his ERA swelled from 2.49 to an ungodly 9.85 as he walked almost exactly one batter per inning. One game into the 1974 season he called it quits.

It's happened to more than one pitcher, too. Rick Ankiel went 11-7 in his first full season, 2000, striking out 10 batters per every nine innings. In the 2000 playoffs, he worked three games, anguished through an ERA of 15.75, and threw nine wild pitches in just four innings. The old "stick a fork in him" line applied—in 2001, he pitched in six games (7.13 ERA), was out all of 2002 with an injury, and never pitched again after his final five bullpen outings in 2004 at the age of 24. He did last in the majors through 2013 after converting to the outfield. He smashed 25 homers one year, but ended as a .240 hitter.

There's a sort of car crash fascination for fans in such inexplicable cases. Baseball people compare the inability to make routine throws to golfers' yips, a condition in which even a pro finds what should be rote actions to be challenging.

Hall of Fame shortstop Alan Trammell said most infielders will typically commit about 15 errors per year—that comes with the territory—but when that number reaches up to 25 or so, something is wrong. However, second baseman Steve Sax was guilty of a personal high of 30 errors with many coming on those so-called routine lobs to first. The sudden onset of the inability to make accurate throws applies not exclusively to pitchers. Some call this condition the Steve Sax Syndrome.

Teammate Pedro Guerrero, himself a shaky-fielding third baseman, found humor in Sax's plight once. He was asked what goes through his mind when he was in the field. He said he thought two things. "First, please don't hit the ball to me. Second, please don't hit it to Sax."

A few other fielders suffered through Sax-like woes, including Chuck Knoblauch, Dale Murphy when he was a catcher, and another catcher, Mackey Sasser. He had difficulties making the shortest of throws—the routine return lob back to the pitcher. He even sought help from psychiatrists and hypnotists, but nothing worked. His issue first surfaced in 1987, and despite his mental block, he lasted until early in the 1995 season. When it came time to throw out would be base stealers, his success percentage was just a bit below league average.

Chapter 6

Humor and the Lighter Side of the Game

Baseball is a game rich with old tales involving humor—remember the title of Joe Garagiola's book, *Baseball Is a Funny Game*. Quite a bit of the laughs baseball has given us come from deprecating, biting, and/or gallows humor.

Consider the time slick-fielding Larry Bowa cleverly insulted his rival shortstop Dave Concepción, who had been experiencing a very uncharacteristic streak of fielding misplays. Before a game, Bowa approached Concepción and said, "I never knew your first name was Elmer." A perplexed Concepción said, "Why do you ask that? You know my name is Dave." Bowa replied, "Every time I look at the box score I see E Concepción."

One pitcher got saddled with a permanent, derogatory nickname. Hugh Mulcahy earned the label "Losing Pitcher." And, yes, he did fit the description. His lifetime record stood at 45-89, he twice led his league in earned runs allowed and in losses when he lost 20 or more games, he never enjoyed a winning season, and his career ERA was 4.49. Despite his inefficiency, he endured for nine seasons, between 1935 and 1947.

His nickname stemmed from sportswriters joking that in box scores they often saw "LP" next to his name, so they added "Losing Pitcher" as a supplement to his real name. Despite all of that, he made the NL All-Star team in 1940.

Fierce competitor Bob Gibson was experiencing an unusually tough inning one day, so his catcher, Tim McCarver, decided to pay him a mound visit. Bad idea. Gibson promptly dismissed him, telling him to get back behind the plate, doing so with a scathing, "The only thing you know about pitching is how hard it is to hit."

Dizzy Dean sent a message to a young hitter who had just stepped into the box to face him. "Son," he said, "What kind of pitch would you like to miss?" Another time Dean made fun of himself when he spoke about how he had dropped out of school in second grade. He commented, "I didn't do so well in first grade, either."

One creative vandal evoked laughter in Philadelphia in 1936. During that period of time when the Phillies were pathetic, a sign in the outfield advertised a brand of soap, touting, "The Phillies Use Lifebuoy." Someone with a barbed sense of humor added to the sign, "And they still stink!" They did. In the 11 years the sign was up, the team finished last or next-to-last eight times.

In Harold Rosenthal's *The 10 Best Years of Baseball*, he wrote about an argument reporters had—should they announce the paid attendance for each game or the total heads in the ballpark? One writer argued for the number of fans who actually showed up for the game. "If they dropped an atomic bomb on the joint," he began, "would it get everyone or just those who had bought tickets?"

Whitey Herzog was once negotiating his next managerial contract with Cardinals owner August Busch, then 85 years old. Busch wanted to keep the highly successful Herzog around so he offered him a lifetime contract. Herzog, no dummy, asked, "Whose lifetime, yours or mine?"

When Texas catcher Rich Billings saw he was slotted to hit sixth in an upcoming game, he complained to manager Billy Martin. "I was hitting fourth when Whitey Herzog was managing." Martin was quick with his comeback, "Maybe that's the reason Herzog isn't managing here anymore."

Pitcher Kirby Higbe was deathly afraid of flying. On one team flight his Dodger teammate Pee Wee Reese tried to console him, assuring him that there was no need to worry because when a person's number is up, it doesn't matter if you're in the air or on the ground. Higbe wasn't at all swayed by such logic. "Suppose I'm up here with a pilot, and my number isn't up, but *his* is."

In Hank Aguirre's 1955 major-league debut, the third batter he faced was Ted Williams. Aguirre struck him out en route to his first win. He then ventured into the Boston clubhouse and approached the superstar, asking for an autograph on the ball he had used for his memorable strikeout. They say Williams stared at the youngster for a moment, probably fuming inside. Still, he did oblige Aguirre.

Three years later Williams got his revenge, pulling a pitch for a long home run. As the story goes, as Williams triumphantly toured the bases, he sneered at the rookie on the mound. "Hey, kid," Williams snorted, "go get that ball and I'll sign it for you, too."

Babe Herman was infamous for his futile outfield play. One time he misplayed a flyball, coming in on the ball, then back, then slipping on the grass. He got back up, chased the ball to the fence, fumbled and even kicked the ball around a bit. Finally, if the legend is true, he threw the ball over the backstop. Later, when asked by a reporter what happened, he replied, "When?" The thing is, even if this story is apocryphal, it's still a great part of baseball lore.

In the fantastic book *The Pitcher*, there's a story of a rookie who was asked why he hadn't used the rosin bag. His reply was, "I couldn't get it open."

Next, a classic tale about heavy drinker Hack Wilson. One day his manager Joe McCarthy wanted to get a point across about how alcohol hurts a player's performance. So with Wilson looking on, he dropped a worm into a glass of water, then after a few seconds he rescued the worm, alive and wiggling. Next, he plopped it into a glass of whiskey. The worm quickly died. His point apparently made, McCarthy asked Wilson if he had learned a lesson. Wilson replied, yes, "It means that if I keep on drinking liquor, I ain't going to have no worms."

Another manager, Casey Stengel, had some miscommunication with one of his players, Mickey McDermott, after catching him trying to sneak into the team hotel after hitting some bars until 4:00 a.m. Stengel gazed at McDermott coldly and declared, "Drunk again!" McDermott grinned, "Me, too."

A young Marty Marion was negotiating a contract with baseball executive Branch Rickey, a notoriously tight-fisted front office man. Marion let Rickey know he was none too pleased at what he was offering. After going back and forth a bit, Rickey said that if Marion would just accept his proposed salary, he would make it up to him later. "I'll take care of you," Rickey promised. Marion shot back, "Give me what I want, and I'll take care of myself."

Andy Van Slyke came up with a good one soon after he first joined the Orioles. He was informed that his new team did not permit players to have any hair below the lip. He quipped, "Does that mean I have to shave my legs?"

Speaking of hair, Rollie Fingers sported a handlebar mustache. A writer referenced a famous commercial featuring Joe Namath shaving off his mustache for a company which manufactured shaving cream. Namath received $10,000 for taking part in the commercial. The writer asked Fingers if he would shave off his mustache for such a payday. Fingers replied, "For $10,000 I'd grow one on my butt."

Even the Hall of Fame, an august organization, has a sense of baseball humor. In 2017, they "inducted" Homer Simpson to

VILLAGE OF COOPERSTOWN
PROCLAMATION
HOMER SIMPSON DAY
MAY 27, 2017

WHEREAS, Homer J. Simpson of Springfield, has, in a lifetime of superior achievement, gone to space, won a Grammy, climbed the Murderhorn, won a Pulitzer Prize and saved his hometown from nuclear meltdowns, and,

WHEREAS, Homer J. Simpson has contributed to baseball history, first as Dancin' Homer, the official mascot of the Springfield Isotopes, and, then, as hero of the Springfield Nuclear Power Plant softball team, driving in the game winning run with his heads up play in the 1992 championship game vs. Shelbyville,

THEREFORE, in honor of his service to baseball and this country, I proclaim today, May 27, 2017, Homer J. Simpson Day in Cooperstown.

Jeff Katz, Mayor
Village of Cooperstown

In 2017, Homer Simpson was "inducted" into the Hall of Fame, commemorating the 25th anniversary of a *Simpsons* episode, "Homer at the Bat." FROM THE COLLECTION OF JEFF KATZ

commemorate the 25th anniversary of a baseball-themed episode, "Homer at the Bat."

Jeff Katz said, "That was the best. When the story came out that the Hall was going to 'induct' Homer Simpson, Jeff Idelson was president of the Hall and I was mayor." Katz wrote up a proclamation "declaring Homer Simpson Day and read it at the event." He did so while "wearing a big sash like Mayor Quimby [of the cartoon] does. I read it straight, like it wasn't a joke. Some of the guys who were in 'Homer at the Bat' were there: Steve Sax, Ozzie Smith, and Wade Boggs."

In 1985, Jack Clark was traded from the Giants to the Cardinals for four players, including José González. Not long into that year, González had his surname legally changed to Uribe. That led to one observer stating González was "the ultimate player to be named later."

Who can forget Morgana Roberts, known as "The Kissing Bandit," a fan of quite a few players who was also a self-promoter. Her sort of sideshow act was to go onto fields and interrupt the game's action by providing her own somewhat steamy action, smooching hand-picked ballplayers. Her distracting, intrusive act began in 1969, when the exotic dancer pranced onto the diamond and got instant publicity and notoriety by planting a kiss on Pete Rose's cheek (many years later she would kiss Pete Rose Jr.). In a decidedly huge understatement, she once said that the players seemed to notice her. Gee, wonder why?

Her measurements, far more interesting than the ballpark's dimensions, stacked up at a hard-to-believe 60-23-39. Later, some minor-league teams hired her to kiss a player to entertain their fans, a far cry from the days when she was arrested 19 times.

Then there are celeb/fans like Larry King (who wrote a book about his love for the game), an omnipresent figure behind home plate at Dodger Stadium, sitting near Mary Hart, a host on *Entertainment*

Tonight. Manager Tommy Lasorda even arranged for her to sing the National Anthem at the park once.

She has been a season ticket holder for an eternity and a true fan for more than 40 years. That's totally unlike the celebrities who are trotted out by a network such as Fox when they cover a World Series game—the ones who are then focused on by the TV camera to hype their Fox show only to disappear from the park shortly after their cameo appearance.

Hart got serious TV exposure when she imitated Craig Kimbrel's peculiar stance as he gazed in from the mound to get his catcher's sign. He resembled a man squatting with his arms hooked in a position that seemed like an imitation of an albatross with its wings partially outstretched.

Some other celebrities who are legitimate fans include comedians Kevin James, Jerry Seinfeld, Billy Crystal, and Jon Lovitz; actors Jon Hamm, Ben Affleck, Tom Hanks, Bill Murray, Alyssa Milano, Vince Vaughn, Charlie Sheen, Jennifer Lopez, and Chris Pratt; and musicians Garth Brooks and Jay-Z.

Big political figures who loved baseball include George W. Bush, who was once a partial owner of the Texas Rangers, his father George H. W. who played college ball at Yale, Ronald Reagan who once broadcast Chicago Cubs games, re-creating the action over the airwaves as messaged to him remotely from a telegrapher who was attending the actual games, and Barack Obama.

Some players are, or were, married to famous women, including Justin Verlander with Kate Upton, a model; Nomar Garciaparra and Mia Hamm, soccer star; and, of course there's Joe DiMaggio who was married to Marilyn Monroe.

Then there were the colorful owners who provided offbeat and lighthearted moments. Charlie Finley once had his starting lineup chauffeured onto the field prior to a game in a limousine. Another time he had his starters ride into the ballpark on a mule train. He was also believed to be the man responsible for the idea of using orange baseballs in a game.

All-Star pitcher Clyde Wright said his main memory of Finley was of "that damned orange ball because I gave up seven runs one day experimenting with that thing [in spring training].

"It was terrible. I think Catfish Hunter pitched in that game and he didn't like it, either. The ball was too slick. They said they wanted the hitters to see the ball better. If they saw it any better, the pitchers wouldn't have a job," he concluded.

Actually, orange balls had been used earlier, as an experiment back in August of 1938. The trial lasted for only one game and was shelved.

Joe Engel, owner of the Chattanooga Lookouts, also craved attention for his team, and he knew showcasing fascinating gate attractions was one way of getting it. Steve Martini wrote about some of the promotions such as the time Engel announced the next game would feature a raffle to win a house. That drew an overflow crowd to the park including fans who were permitted to sit on the field along the outfield walls. Not wanting to pay for baseballs that might become souvenirs for the fans, he froze the game balls, making them unlikely to be hit too deeply.

He once pulled off a trade in which he sent a player to a Charlotte team for a 25-pound turkey and exclaimed, "The turkey was having a better year." Another time he pulled off an Elephant Hunt which was nothing more than allowing fans a chance to "hunt" papier-mâché animals in the outfield.

He signed a 17-year-old girl named Jackie Mitchell to pitch an exhibition game versus the Yankees in 1931. The Lookouts starter gave up a double and a single to open the game. It was then that the southpaw Mitchell took to the mound and promptly struck out Babe Ruth and Lou Gehrig, each going down on three pitches. Tony Lazzeri walked and Mitchell then departed with the starter reentering the contest. Now, some say the Yankee sluggers went along with the gimmick, originally slated to be played on April Fool's Day, but pushed back a day due to rain.

Mitchell became the first woman to sign an organized baseball contract (which was voided several days after her performance) in the modern era. She went on to barnstorm and even played for the House of David, a team famous for its barnstorming tours and the fact that its players all had beards—well, almost all of them, and Mitchell wasn't the only exception. Big leaguers sometimes joined the team, including Satchel Paige and Grover Cleveland Alexander, and they had the choice of growing facial hair or wearing a fake beard. Still, the question remains: Did the stars strike out on purpose against Mitchell? Nobody knows for sure.

What we do know is softball pitcher Jenny Finch, an Olympic champion, whiffed a boatload of big leaguers including Albert Pujols. Watching her puzzle stars on the internet with her balls' speed and movement was an incredible sight.

Some playful ballplayers enrich the game, too. Ozzie Smith's handsprings stand out, but many other players had noteworthy mannerisms like those who go through a routine or ritual when they're in the batter's box. Former catcher Joe Torre played with and against Rico Carty and remembered, "He was very religious or superstitious. He used to draw a cross with his bat at home plate, and I used to erase it. It really irritated him, so he'd keep doing it and I'd keep erasing it, just kidding with him."

Torre also pointed out some of Tito Fuentes's ways. "He did the baton twirl with his bat. He'd bounce it off home plate then flamboyantly catch the spinning bat." And Willie Stargell turned his bat into a propeller, looping it in large windmill circles almost up until the moment that the pitch was heading his way.

Hall of Fame second baseman Joe Morgan had his little chicken flap move he'd do with his front arm, slapping it against his torso. Mike Hargrove said, "Every time I saw him do that, I thought it was something to remind him to keep his elbow down."

Wade Boggs believed in superstitions the way Newton believed in gravity. Even his plaque at Cooperstown mentioned his legendary superstitious ways. Just a few of Boggs's good-luck methods: He used to take his bat and scrawl *chai*, a Hebrew word which translates to "good luck and life" in the dirt of the batter's box, he earned the nickname "Chicken Man" for his habit of eating chicken before every game, and he took precisely 150 grounders in practice daily.

Former Toronto manager Cito Gaston recalled slugger Albert Belle's habits. "He looks like he kind of lines himself up in the batter's box by putting one foot in front of the other. Then he backs off and draws a line in the dirt."

Chapter 7

Baseball Players as Fans

Some of the game's most appreciative fans are the players themselves. Former big leaguer Bill Haselman said there are more fans of baseball than just those in the stands. "I think the players were all fans of the game before we ever played it."

Ron Blomberg sounded more like a fan than a player when he gushed about his former team. "I was on the best team ever and was in the greatest organization in the game of baseball with the New York Yankees. I got to play for the team that I wanted to play for. George Steinbrenner would always tell you, 'When you wore the Yankee pinstripes, you wore it with honor.' I got to play in Yankee Stadium, and I got to wear the pinstripes. How much more could you want?"

Roger Clemens spent time with the Yankees and was a fan of Babe Ruth. Julia Ruth Stevens, the daughter of the Babe, said, "He always patted Daddy's memorial in Monument Park before he went in to pitch."

Players are even appreciative fans of other players, be they teammates or opponents. Andre Dawson heaped praise on Fred McGriff back when they were active players. "He amazes me because he doesn't even seem to swing very hard and the ball jumps off his bat. Most of his home runs are tape-measure shots, and when he's swinging the bat real well, he's a joy to watch."

An old commercial stated that "chicks dig the long ball." Well, so do ballplayers. Mickey Tettleton loved watching McGriff, "The Crime Dog," put a hurt on the ball. "He hits them where most guys need a driver or a three wood to get to."

Paul Molitor will forever remember one home run, a Tettleton blast at Tiger Stadium. "He went way over the roof in right field in Tiger Stadium. He's one of not too many left handers to do that." There had only been 14 such homers hit at that point. "I respect his power from both sides of the plate, but he's more awesome probably from the left side."

Sparky Anderson was in awe watching Albert Belle, the only man with 50+ doubles and 50 or more homers in a season (1995). Anderson said, "When he connects . . ." then he paused looking for an apt finish, but could only come up with, "*Whew*!"

Joe Carter, who gave us an iconic moment with his World Series–winning home run in 1993, couldn't believe a shot hit by Kevin Mitchell. "He hit one in San Diego down the line, up in the second deck. I've never seen anyone go up there. Nobody came close. He just golfed it some 450 feet away!"

Yet another fan of long homers was, of all things, a victimized pitcher. Nolan Ryan gave up a mammoth homer once but still looked back upon it with a sense of awe and appreciation. "The longest one I ever gave up in Arlington was the one Bo Jackson hit to center field. I think it was the longest one they ever measured there."

Dave Winfield said he just had to be impressed with Cecil Fielder "going over the stand in Milwaukee [at old County Stadium] and onto roof tops." Molitor added, "Cecil is the only guy in my history in Milwaukee to go *over* the bleachers."

Catcher Rick Dempsey has that 1991 shot embedded in his mind, too. "It was the longest ball I ever saw. He hit it out of the entire stadium. Dan Plesac threw him a fastball and it just disappeared into the night. I looked up to see the fans and who was going to catch it, but they were all just looking up, too." Dempsey said the baseball traveled 30 feet above the 8-foot fence just beyond the top row of seats in left field, "and that's a conservative estimate. It went halfway up the light tower there," he concluded.

The titanic shot finally came to rest in the parking lot about 520 feet from home plate, and it's said to be the only ball ever driven completely out of that venue.

Dawson was taken with Andrés Galarraga's might. "He's strong! I've seen some of the home runs he's hit and some were tape measure jobs. He's a guy you can make a mistake with and he can lose a ball."

Dawson concluded his peer evaluation with his take on Dave Justice. "He has that real nice and easy stroke, and the ball just seems to jump off his bat. He's one of the bigger guys, and with that stroke, he generates a lot of bat speed." And power—Justice crushed 305 lifetime home runs.

Appreciative players who also are big baseball fans are impressed by more than just power displays. All-Star second baseman Carlos Baerga said he'll never forget a defensive jewel—actually, two. "I saw triple plays against Boston when Minnesota turned two in the same game." That marked the first time such rare plays ever happened in a big-league game, and both went around the horn.

"I thought that was the most amazing thing I ever saw in my life. It went Gary Gaetti, to Al Newman, to Kent Hrbek."

Former manager Terry Collins also went with a fielding beauty. "Probably the most amazing play that I saw personally was the play Moisés Alou made when he was playing center field for me in Buffalo. A ball was hit over his head and he caught it on the dead run, stretched out, diving away from home plate. Unbelievable play!" He compared it to the unforgettable over-the-head snag by Willie Mays in the 1954 World Series, but pointed out Mays stayed on his feet while Alou made a diving snatch. "When Alou reached out and caught it with one hand, I couldn't even believe he got *near* the ball."

Dave Winfield was stunned by what Yankee teammate Don Mattingly did in 1987. "He hit six grand slams in one year, a record, and all of them right in front of me in the batting order, so I had a front row seat. He really cleared the bases—he had 24 RBI on six at bats!" An unbelievable 21 percent of his 115 runs driven in that year came on just six trips to the plate. Cleveland's Travis Hafner tied the single-season slam record in 2006. Amazingly, Mattingly's six grand slams were the only ones he would record over his 14-year career. Hafner totaled 12 in his 12 big-league seasons.

Winfield could have tossed in Mattingly's record-tying eight straight games hitting a homer. That remains tied with Dale Long and Ken Griffey Jr. In another entry on baseball's long list of coincidences, Griffey began his streak in a game in which Mattingly also homered.

Hall of Fame hurler John Smoltz appreciated speed on the basepaths, recalling "when Otis Nixon and Deion Sanders batted one-two in Chicago. Otis was on first and Deion hit either a flare or a flyball that dropped in, and it was the fastest I've ever seen two runners round the bases. And there were errors on the play, so they just kept going, one base after another, like rabbits getting chased. I mean they did it with *extreme* speed!"

Players say they appreciate the beauty of ballparks—they may be where they go to make a living, but that doesn't prevent them from enjoying the aesthetics of the old ballyard. Three-time Gold Glove winner Darin Erstad said that based on a park's looks, his favorite venue was (what's now called old) Yankee Stadium. "That's a no-brainer," he said.

Another veteran catcher, Rod Barajas, agreed, saying he most appreciates the old, venerable parks. "I like [old] Yankee Stadium and I like Dodgers Stadium. I grew up in L.A. so I absolutely love going to Dodger games; and just the history of Yankee Stadium."

Phil Nevin, who went along with Barajas about loving old parks such as Fenway and Wrigley, said, "Of the newer, more modern parks, I would say Jacobs Field is one of the better looking ones and the one in Pittsburgh [PNC Park]."

Tom Grieve opined, "I guess Baltimore. It sticks out in my mind. It's a newer park, but it's still got the old-fashioned look. It has the barbecue out in right field and the fans walking around out there. Of the more modern [looking] ones, I like Seattle and Houston."

In 2006, Paul Byrd opted for several parks: "I love Wrigley Field just because of the history behind it, there's something special there. I really like Baltimore; esthetically it's one of my tops, it's got a great, great feel. I like this field here [Jacobs Field, now Progressive Field] because of the huge scoreboard in left field—I like the feel of the scoreboard and the drama. And the background—it's a great place to pitch. San Francisco has a neat field, it's just unique."

Outfielder Ryan Church said he enjoys playing in the "great fields that have some history," adding that players do care, at least somewhat, about the aesthetics of their surroundings. "It's nice to go in and take it all in, but a park's a park." He reached that bottom line because hitters are ultimately more concerned about dimensions than beauty. In 2005, he said of his home park, Washington's RFK Stadium, "You'd rather have it be like a bandbox, a hitters' park, but it's not, it's a pitchers' park. But a lot of places we go to, it's beautiful, and they're all brand new. Usually they're hitters' parks, so we tend to like that. In all the new ones, the balls fly."

Bill Haselman had great views of the ballparks he played in, squatting behind the plate for 13 seasons. By 2000, he knew that many of the old venues were being razed. "I hate to see old things ripped down because they're a part of history. So many great things happened in those places and then they're gone.

"I played in Fenway for three years and I hate to see the day when that thing goes. So much history there."

Gabe Kapler was an outfielder for 12 years and, through 2023, he had managed in the majors for another six seasons. He is yet another man who has often taken in the beauty of ballparks. "I've done that like the first time I was in Yankee Stadium and Fenway [in 1998], and parks like that. I went around and checked them out. They're pretty enjoyable because you've seen them on TV. So, yeah, I am a fan."

Finally, some records set were so special they left even normally hardened players with goosebumps. The 1941 Yankees were such a juggernaut they rolled to the pennant with ease, clinching it earlier than any other team ever managed. Their players knew they were headed to the Fall Classic as early as September 4, not long after Labor Day.

Likewise, one team won so methodically, they wound up leaving the second-place team as a mere dot in their dust, visible only slightly through their rearview mirror. The 1902 Pirates finished atop the NL by a cozy cushion of 27½ games. Imagine the joy of following that team all season long.

A few other fantastic records that wowed even the players:

- The 2007 Texas Rangers set two nine-inning records when they plastered 30 runs on the board against Baltimore, and by creating the largest margin of victory ever, coasting to a 27-run advantage.
- The 1916 New York Giants went through two long stretches where nobody, but nobody, could beat them. True, they began

the season at 2-13, but they then reeled off 17 consecutive wins. Down the stretch run, they also enjoyed a stupendous 26-game win streak.

Now come the kickers: (1) the 17-game skein came entirely on a road trip; (2) the 26-game spree came on a l—o—n—g home stand—you never see such interminable home stands any more; (3) despite the long streaks, the Giants finished in fourth place, seven games behind Brooklyn. Even when they lifted their record from 59-61 with the 26-game splurge, they couldn't get out of the hole they dug with their previous losing ways—they began the streak in fourth place and didn't budge an inch from there; they didn't gain ground on anybody.

- The longest game ever played in the majors ran a grueling 26 innings and ended in a 1–1 Dead Ball Era tie due to darkness in the days before ballparks had lighting. It took place on May 1, 1920, and this one has some astonishing kickers, too:

  (1) That marathon took just 3 hours and 50 minutes to play. By way of contrast, the season before new rules to speed the game up were put into play in 2023, games ran 3 hours and about 4 minutes, and the contests which stretched to four hours got little if any notice. The 26-inning game clocked out at about four-and-a-half minutes per every half inning.

  (2) And this is the most incredible fact of all, especially to today's fans—both starting pitchers went the distance. Leon Cadore of the Dodgers and Joe Oeschger of the Braves battled on and on, more than satisfying those who love pitchers' duels, even if, at the same time it both amazed and drained players and fans alike.

(3) Another fact to stun modern fans—Oeschger estimated he threw about 250 pitches while Cadore guessed it took him nearly 300 pitches to go the route. All that work for nothing in a way—neither got a decision.

Cadore pitched to 95 batters, fewer than four hitters each inning, and Oeschger did even better, facing only 90 men. Cadore set a record by registering 13 assists, more than any pitcher in a single game ever (his opponent racked up 11 assists). Oeschger established a new record by working 21 straight shutout innings in a game, one better than Cadore. Boston's first baseman, Walter Holke, was particularly busy with 32 putouts and an assist. Only three Dodgers reached as far as third base—the runner who scored and two men who were wiped out on double play action according to author Norman L. Macht.

The game would not have been so memorable except for an error by Oeschger which allowed the Dodgers' only run of the game to score. Take that away and Oeschger wins a 1–0 contest in nine innings and many entries in the record books would never have been written.

Macht wrote in the book *The Ol' Ball Game* that when Cadore was being attended to by a doctor in 1958, the physician complained to him that he couldn't locate a good vein for a needle. He said, "A man your age should have a vein sticking right out, especially in that right arm that pitched those 26 innings." Cadore smiled and replied, "Doc, I pitched that game with my head."

Cadore later stated that his arm was so sore he couldn't even comb his hair for three days. Still, a week later he resumed his turn in the rotation. He also said that he had never before had a sore arm and that he never again came up sore. However, he added that he never again "had the same stuff." In fact, he ended the season at 15-14 but his win totals over the next few years tapered off to 13, eight, four, then zero. His career was over at the end of his winless 1924 season. He wound up with 68 wins, 72 losses, and one unforgettable no decision.

Oeschger's career path was rather similar although after going 15-13 in 1920, he followed that up with a 20-win season. Then he hit the skids, winning only six, five, four, then in his final season, just one victory while wearing the uniform of the team he had baffled for 26 innings, Brooklyn. Like Cadore, he also wound up with a sub-.500 career mark at 82-116. Still, what he and Cadore did on May 1, 1920, forever remains etched in the record books.

For the record, the minors once had a game which stretched to 33 innings over two days involving Cal Ripken Jr. and his Rochester Red Wings and Wade Boggs with his Pawtucket Red Sox. The game was postponed at 4:00 a.m. during the early hours of Easter Sunday and resumed later, when the teams met again on June 23.

Chapter 8

Baseball and the Media

Books

Publishers have churned out countless books featuring plenty of photos of ballparks. An excellent one compares ballparks to *Green Cathedrals*. Others I'd recommend are *The Ballparks*, *Diamonds*, and *Ballparks Yesterday & Today*.

Some excellent anthologies include any of the editions of *The Fireside Book of Baseball* and *The Armchair Book of Baseball*. Must reading also includes anything written by Bill James and Leonard Koppett.

As for the all-time greats, a hand-picked list of a few of the many classics includes *Eight Men Out*, *Veeck as in Wreck*, *Ball Four*, *Babe* (by Robert Creamer), *The Glory of Their Times*, and *Baseball When the Grass Was Real*. There are too many others to mention, but a pretty good list can be found in yet another book, *501 Baseball Books Fans Must Read Before They Die*.

TV Shows

Two classic TV shows worth noting are *The Baseball Bunch*, which featured Johnny Bench and the San Diego Chicken, and *This Week in Baseball* with Mel Allen and later others such as Ozzie Smith and Warner Fusselle.

Seinfeld character George Costanza was working for Yankee owner George Steinbrenner in quite a few episodes of the sitcom. And former Yankee Jim Bouton starred in the short-lived show (only five episodes aired) *Ball Four*, which shared a title with his controversial 1970 tell-all book.

Baseball even found its way into pop culture with *Saturday Night Live*'s Garrett Morris portraying fictional baseball player Chico Escuela, spouting his trademark line, "Baseball been berry, berry good to me!"

Many ballplayers from Hank Aaron to Ken Griffey Jr. have appeared on sitcoms playing themselves. With Aaron having played in Milwaukee for the Braves, it was only natural that the producer of *Happy Days*, set in that city, had him appear on the program and meet Richie Cunningham.

Advertising

Baseball infiltrates the media, even popping up in commercials. Who can forget Bob Uecker sitting in "the front row." Or Uecker and a whole pack of others such as Billy Martin (making fun of his argumentative ways), Marv Throneberry, and Yogi Berra in the numerous Miller Lite commercials. A common thread in that campaign was a debate—not as serious as nature versus nurture, but less filling versus tastes great.

Around 1975, an auto manufacturer decided to align their product to all-American imagery using a catchy slogan and jingle, "Baseball, hot dogs, apple pie, and Chevrolet." That same company commissioned a Robert Thom painting, *The Mighty Babe,* for use in a print ad. It depicted Ruth's "Called Shot" in the 1932 World Series with him pointing two fingers toward center field before homering.

Many experts dismiss him actually predicting his homer, but in a 2004 interview, his daughter, Julia Ruth Stevens, hoped to settle the matter by saying, "He did hold up his hand. Now what's controversial about that?" Even if he didn't call his shot, it will forever remain in baseball lore (myth?) and that may be the most important thing about it.

TV viewers got to know another slogan quite well after being exposed to Nike's "Bo [Jackson] knows."

People also got to know pitcher Jim Palmer—a whole lot of him—when he was a pitchman for Jockey underwear while wearing nothing else but a pair of that product.

Print Media Quotes

> "The fundamental truth: a baseball game is nothing but a great slow contraption for getting you to pay attention to the cadence of a summer day."—Michael Chabon in *Summerland*

> "The first books I was interested in were all about baseball."—Charles Kuralt

> "Baseball is not a conventional industry. It belongs neither to the players nor management, but to all of us. It is our national pastime, our national symbol, and our national treasure."—John Thorn in *Baseball: Our Game*

"It's America, this baseball. A reissued newsreel of boyhood dreams. Dreams lost somewhere between boy and man. . . . And a rock home plate and a chicken wire backstop—anywhere."—Ernie Harwell in *The Game for All America* (reading this entire essay is highly recommended).

"Since baseball time is measured only in outs, all you have to do is succeed utterly; keep hitting, keep the rally alive, and you have defeated time. You remain forever young."—Roger Angell in *The Summer Game*

"Baseball is a universal language. Catch the ball, throw the ball, hit the ball."—Pete Rose in *My Prison Without Bars*

"Baseball is the most perfect of games, solid, true, pure and precious as diamonds. If only life were so simple."—W. P. Kinsella in *Shoeless Joe*

"You spend a good piece of your life gripping a baseball and in the end it turns out it was the other way around all the time."—Jim Bouton in *Ball Four*

"Baseball players are smarter than football players. How often do you see a baseball team penalized for too many men on the field?"—Bouton in *Ball Four*

"Baseball is a drama with an endless run and an ever-changing cast."—Joe Garagiola in *Baseball Is A Funny Gam*e

"Wonderboy flashed in the sun. It caught the sphere where it was the biggest. A noise like a twenty-one gun salute cracked the sky." —Bernard Malamud in *The Natural*

"Baseball is an American icon. It is the Statue of Liberty, the bald eagle, 'In God We Trust,' Mount Rushmore, ice cream, apple pie, hot dogs, and rally monkeys. Baseball is America." —Victor Baltov Jr. in *Baseball Is America*

"It breaks your heart. It is designed to break your heart. The game begins in the spring, when everything else begins again, and it blossoms in the summer, filling the afternoons and evenings, and then as soon as the chill rains come, it stops and leaves you to face the fall alone." —A. Bartlett Giamatti in *A Great and Curious Game*

Movies

There has been a seemingly infinite number of movies with a baseball theme or tie-in, too many to cover, so here's a small sampling.

Begin with *The Natural*, which has its share of memorable scenes. Who can forget Roy Hobbs's smash which demolishes the park's light standards, setting off a wondrous pyrotechnic display accompanied by a climactic musical crescendo. In an art-following-life scenario, the Hobbs homer is reminiscent of Reggie Jackson's mammoth home run, which traveled 539 feet at the 1971 All-Star Game in Tiger Stadium. The ball would have cleared the roof looming there had it not banged into a transformer housed on top of the stands.

Angels in the Outfield was released in 1951, and another version, produced by Walt Disney Pictures, came out 43 years later. It's not every college kid who gets the opportunity to appear in a major Hollywood release, but baseball gave that chance to a University of Pittsburgh student. Bill Priatko, a member of the Panthers football squad, accepted a small role playing the Pittsburgh Pirates' center fielder in the original, MGM production of the movie starring Paul Douglas.

"We filmed for two weeks at Forbes Field," recalled Priatko, "It was a heck of an experience. We used to sit in the dugout and talk with Pie Traynor—he had a different humorous baseball story to tell every day. He was a great guy. And I got to know the Hollywood movie stars like Janet Leigh."

A 1989 release, *The Dream Team*, starred Michael Keaton, who was joined in the cast by Christopher Lloyd, Peter Boyle, and Stephen Furst as inpatients in a mental institution. They wind up making a supervised field trip into New York City to take in a Yankees game. However, when a doctor who accompanied the group is knocked out and taken to a hospital, the four patients are on their own.

One baseball reference here deals with the character Albert, played by Furst. He communicates with others by using baseball terms, especially those used by Yankees color commentator Phil Rizzuto. Another occurs when a patient is first told that they are going to go to a Yankees ballgame. In amazement, he says, "You mean we are actually leaving the hospital grounds?" Keaton's character sarcastically replies, "No, the Yankees are going to come here and play. They're gonna throw some lights up in the rec room."

Ultimately, the men make it to a game in Yankee Stadium. One critic complained that the film was derivative of *One Flew Over the Cuckoo's Nest*.

Now, that classic movie certainly did relate to the love of baseball. The patients in an institution began listening to the 1963 World Series on the radio. Astute baseball fans recognize they're being treated to Ernie Harwell delivering the account of the game. When Nurse Ratched has the broadcast turned off, it's Jack Nicholson who picks up the slack and provides his own imaginary play-by-play, describing a pitch from Sandy Koufax ripped by Bobby Richardson for a double.

Major League, like *Dream Team*, was released on April 7, 1989. In fact, at number one at the box office, it opened one slot above *Dream Team* on the list of domestic hits for that weekend's films. Bob Uecker's most famous line, playing the character of broadcaster Harry Doyle, came when he described a very wild pitch from Ricky "Wild Thing" Vaughn as being, "*Juuuuust* a bit outside."

Additional select baseball movies—simply a sampler (some good, some not so good, some funny, some serious): *Eight Men Out*, *Mr. 3,000*, *Cobb*, *Bang the Drum Slowly*, *A League of Their Own*, *The Rookie*, *The Sandlot*, *Brewster's Millions*, *Fear Strikes Out*, *The Pride of St. Louis*, *The Bad News Bears*, *Rookie of the Year*, *61**, *The Kid from Left Field*, *It Happens Every Spring*, *Bingo Long Traveling All-Stars & Motor Kings*, *It's Good to be Alive*, *Rhubarb*, *Damn Yankees*, *Safe at Home*, *The Kid from Cleveland*, *The Stratton Story*, and *Little Big League*—apologies if your favorite was not listed.

Next, some actors who looked believable as ballplayers. Charlie Sheen, who played Vaughn, had a 40-15 record as a high school pitcher. Kevin Costner, who appeared in five movies with baseball themes, including *Field of Dreams*, *Bull Durham*, and *For Love of the Game*, was also a star high school athlete. Incidentally, a Hall of Fame survey conducted in 2003 ranked *Bull Durham* as the best baseball film ever with *Field of Dreams* and *A League of Their Own* far behind.

Publicity photo for the movie *Bull Durham*, voted as the best baseball film ever by far. WIKIMEDIA COMMONS

Tom Selleck actually played in a 1991 exhibition game for the Tigers, his favorite team, as part of his preparation to play in the movie *Mr. Baseball.* Manager Sparky Anderson surprised Selleck by inserting him into the game for a pinch at-bat. He looked pretty good at the plate before fanning on a knuckle-curve.

Stealing Home starred Mark Harmon, who may not have been a baseball star (though he did play the sport in high school), but he was very convincing as an athlete. Harmon's father Tom won the Heisman Trophy, while Mark was UCLA's quarterback and won 17 games and lost only five.

A few of the worst jobs of trying to look athletic were turned in by Anthony Perkins who portrayed Jimmy Piersall, and a future US president, Ronald Reagan, playing the role of pitcher Grover Alexander in *The Winning Team*, looking herky-jerky in his delivery despite editing efforts. Casting a clumsy-looking Gary Cooper as Lou Gehrig in *Pride of the Yankees* was a big mistake.

Then there were the laughable, but not intentionally so, ones. John Goodman in *The Babe* and William Bendix in *The Babe Ruth Story* tried to emulate the incomparable hitter. By the way, Ruth himself should have stuck to playing baseball, not acting in baseball films—he appeared in 10 films counting short ones. In one role the makeup was terrible, making him look pasty faced.

Next, the documentaries. One "must" is a series of three superb documentaries, *When It Was a Game* and its two sequels. Of course Ken Burns's epic *Baseball* is a more well known classic. Another top-notch documentary is *Battered Bastards of Baseball* with Kurt Russell (who once played Double-A ball). Sidenote: Kurt's father, Bing, who owned the minor-league team featured in the movie, also has a grandson who made it to the majors, Matt Franco. A few other documentaries of note: *Facing Nolan*, *Screwball*, *Ballplayer: Pelotero*, and *Four Days in October.*

There are at least six movies focusing on Jackie Robinson including the excellent *42* and *The Jackie Robinson Story* with Robinson playing himself. In this case, he naturally did a more convincing job of looking like a ballplayer than an accomplished actor.

Many ballplayers appear in movies more or less as extras, portraying players but often having no lines, while others make cameo appearances, such as a short scene with Roger Maris and Mickey Mantle in the Doris Day/Cary Grant movie *That Touch of Mink*. Bill Mazeroski agreed to hit into a triple play against the Mets in the film *The Odd Couple*. *Fever Pitch* cameos were turned in by Trot Nixon, Jason Varitek, and Johnny Damon. Finally, Ken Griffey Jr. (and quite a few other big leaguers) were in *Little Big League*. Keith Hernandez, who played himself on *Seinfeld*, also played himself in a non-baseball movie entitled *The Yards*.

Still Pictures

A few of my favorites include: The image of Willie Mays, back to the camera as he raced deep into spacious center field at the Polo Grounds to make his famous 1954 World Series circus catch . . . Lou Gehrig, head and shoulders bent slightly over a fleet of microphones saying his goodbye to baseball . . . Yogi Berra leaping into the arms of pitcher Don Larsen after the last out of the perfect game in the 1956 World Series . . . Johnny Bench's massive right hand clutching seven baseballs . . . the ever-snarling Ty Cobb sliding viciously into third base . . . any photo of Juan Marichal in his patented high-kick delivery.

My pick as the best baseball still shot ever snapped is the one which won the 1949 Pulitzer Prize for Photography for Nathaniel Fein. It was, in fact, the first picture related to a sport to win that honor. The evocative picture shows Babe Ruth, with somewhat stooped shoulders and requiring a bat to lean on for support, on the day he said farewell

The ever-quotable Yogi Berra—who can forget the classic World Series picture of him leaping into the arms of pitcher Don Larsen after Larsen's perfect game to close out the Series?

to Yankee Stadium. The photograph, *Babe Ruth Bows Out*, is especially creative as Fein, unlike every other photographer except one that day, chose to frame Ruth with his back to the camera, accentuating his jersey number—which the team was retiring that day—no need to see his face. The image also vividly portrayed his frail posture. Ruth would die two months after his last goodbye to the house that he had built.

Poems

The two most famous baseball poems are probably "Casey at the Bat" from 1888 and "Baseball's Sad Lexicon" (1910), known to fans as "Tinker to Evers to Chance." Actor De Wolf Hopper said he recited the Casey poem on stage more than 10,000 times over a 47-year period. Many fans are unaware that the poem had a sequel, "Casey's Revenge" by Grantland Rice, in which mighty Casey delights Mudville fans with a homer that sailed out of sight.

As for the Tinker poem by Franklin Pierce Adams, although the words indicate these men formed a premier double play act, they absolutely were not. In 1908, their D.P. total was a record low for the Cubs franchise, and shortstop Tinker once made 72 errors. This infield trio turned just 54 double plays from 1906 to 1909 even when counting going Evers to Tinker and on to Chance.

A few samples of my favorite baseball poems: Ogden Nash's "Lineup for Yesterday" in which he honors stars from A to Z with witty rhymes—check out C for Cobb, G for Gehrig, H for Hornsby, K for Keller, Y for Young, and (look it up) U for 'Ubell as in Carl Hubbell.

Similarly, Eddie Gold did a great job of wordplay in his *Baseball Rhyme Time*, able to link names like Vida Blue with Big Klu; Ty Cobb rhyming with Rusty Staub; Jimmie Foxx goes with Billy Cox; Hank Aaron is joined with the "Red Baron"; there's Dizzy Dean with Harvey Kuenn; and Branch Rickey with Bill Dickey; he even ran "Leo the Lip," Wally Pipp, and Ewell "The Whip" together.

"The Base Stealer" creates imagery so vivid, one can easily picture Cobb, or Lou Brock, or Rickey Henderson boldly taking a lead off base, balanced yet with muscles coiled, waiting, yet ready to explode on his way to another thrilling steal.

My final choice is another poem by Rice, "Game Called"; one version of the poem was published the day after Babe Ruth's death. It is mournful, a touching tribute to the legend.

Final note: pitcher Miguel Batista wrote poetry (and a novel). The title of a book of his poetry written in Spanish is translated as "Feelings in Black and White." And, reliever Dan Quisenberry had two books of his poems published.

Songs/Music

Baseball and music go together like hot dogs and mustard. A *Washington Post* story mentioned that famous songwriters such as George M. Cohan, Chuck Berry, and Irving Berlin wrote songs dealing with baseball; and big-name singers like Brian Wilson, Frank Sinatra, and Billy Joel have sung such tunes. Of course, some songs are heard so often at ballparks, by extension they've become traditional baseball songs. Consider, for example, "Sweet Caroline," "New York, New York," "Y.M.C.A.," and "Glory Days."

"Talkin' Baseball" extols topics such as the trio of New York's superlative stars who patrolled center field for much of the 50s for the Giants, Yankees, and Brooklyn Dodgers: Willie Mays, Mickey Mantle, and Duke Snider. Singers of "Jolting Joe DiMaggio" belted out that they wanted him on their side and alluded to his 56-game hitting streak. And there's "Centerfield," rich in baseball lyrics. Even a popular tune from 1968, "(Love Is Like A) Baseball Game" by The Intruders, compared love to a baseball game in an extended metaphor—an apt comparison as, to many, baseball *is* a form of love.

When Hank Aaron was closing in on Babe Ruth's career home-run record, pitcher Nellie Briles cashed in on that, singing "Hey Hank," with lyrics asking Hank to please not hit the record breaker off him. And Ernie Harwell wrote the lyrics to the song "Move Over, Babe, Here Comes Henry." Bernie Williams has recorded quite a few songs, and he played his guitar and sang "Take Me Out to the Ballgame" at the Hall of Fame ceremony when fellow Yankee Mariano Rivera was inducted.

Other randomly selected baseball songs (from a very long list) include: the disco song "Charlie Hustle" about Pete Rose, "Did You See Jackie Robinson Hit That Ball?," "Mrs. Robinson," "Say Hey (The Willie Mays Song)," "Brown Eyed Handsome Man," "A Dying Cub Fan's Last Request," and "Van Lingle Mungo."

Perhaps the first time a person working for a baseball team got ejected for his musical taste happened in 1985, when minor-league organist Wilbur Snapp made his displeasure over a call known by playing "Three Blind Mice." Another time a worker pumped that song over the PA system as the day's umps came onto the field. He was tossed from the game before it even started.

At an Omaha Royals game, another organist got the hook for his song selection as an argument was taking place with an ump. His musical selection was the theme song from *The Mickey Mouse Club*.

Then there's players' walk-up music. Ken Oberkfell's last name reminded the Cardinals' organist of Obi-Wan Kenobi, so when the third baseman strolled to the plate, he was greeted by the sounds of the *Star Wars* theme. When he was in his mid-20s, Guardians outfielder Oscar González chose an unusual song to accompany him to the plate, a child's song, the theme to *SpongeBob Squarepants*. He chose that song to symbolize the fact that baseball is, in fact, just a game, and a kids' game at that. That was also true for Gerardo Parra, who chose "Baby Shark" for his walk-up tune, doing so because his two-year-old daughter loved the song.

Pitchers can also have a certain song to accompany them as they enter a game, marching in from the bullpen. That was true for fictional character Ricky Vaughn who was serenaded to the hill to the tune of "Wild Thing." Two of the greatest relievers ever, Mariano Rivera (number one on the all-time save list with 652) and Trevor Hoffman (number two on that list at 601), were heralded into games by the walk-on songs "Enter Sandman" by Metallica and "Hells Bells" by AC/DC respectively. For the record, "Sandman" was first used when Billy Wagner trotted in from the bullpen.

Baseball Cards

What fan didn't collect cards, but when I grew up we didn't protect them as ignorance of the future was bliss. Instead of protecting them with sleeves, we played with the cards. In one game, two kids would each flip one card, allowing it to flutter to the ground. If one card came up on the heads (or image side) and the other child's card landed on the reverse side, heads won and the winner would claim both cards.

Another game usually featured two young boys tossing their card Frisbee-style toward a wall. The boy whose card landed the closest to the wall won the other kid's card. Then there was a game we called topsies in which cards were tossed in the same manner at a wall, but in this case there was no winner until one player's card landed on top of another card. The pot could grow pretty large before the winner snatched them all up.

Of course such games damaged cards and diminished their value. That was also true of the way many kids wedged cards between the spokes of their bicycles to produce a clicking sound.

We did read and consume all of the stats and the informational material on the back of the cards. My friends and I would laugh at how creative the writers had to be when describing not a player such as Hank Aaron—"he led the league again last year in home runs and runs driven in"—but players labeled scrubs back then—"Joe Blow once drew a dramatic walk as a pinch hitter in a 10–1 loss." Worse—"Last season Johnny Journeyman, playing for his sixth minor league team, roomed with Jesse Gonder." To read a real sample, just find any Bob Uecker card! One true example from his 1966 Topps card did point out he was a fine defensive catcher, then added that because of that, "Bob is well-liked by the St. Louis pitching staff."

As a kid, I thought Topps (founded in 1938) was the only company to ever put out baseball cards. Even into my early adulthood, I knew

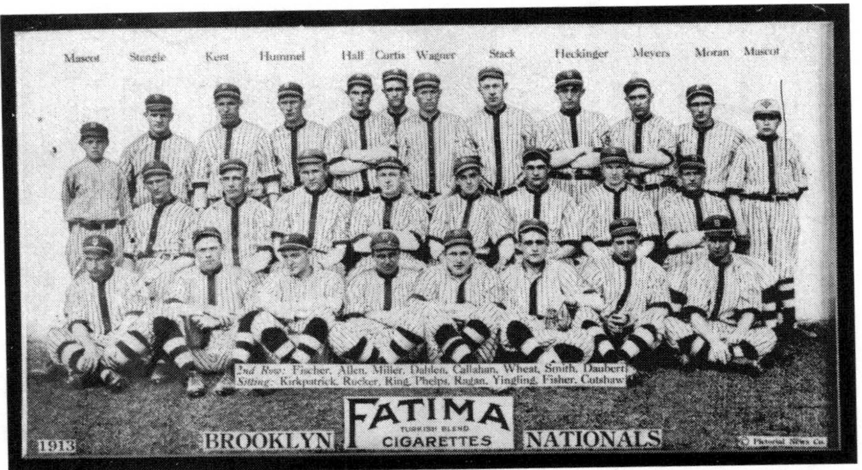

Baseball cards date back to around the time of the Civil War. Here is a team card of the 1913 Brooklyn Dodgers issued long before companies such as Bowman and Topps came along. COURTESY OF THE LIBRARY OF CONGRESS

of only a few companies in that business. Now, thanks to the famous 1911 Honus Wagner American Tobacco card, people are aware of other companies. A few include Goudey, Bowman (which began its operations in 1948), and more recent companies such as Upper Deck, which came along in 1989.

The Hall of Fame has an excellent display of baseball cards going back many decades—stating that card collecting dates back to around the time of the Civil War. The collection of more than 135,000 cards bears the name "The Cards Your Mother Threw Away."

Former Cooperstown mayor Jeff Katz perfectly nailed what many fans feel about card collecting. "It was a constant growing up for me. Baseball cards are where it's at—that's where there is the most history and fun. Everyone tries in their own way to re-capture their own childhood, and cards just bring me right to it." Each card can elicit a memory for him such as, "My wife found the Red Sox Team card and it completed my 1967 set, stories like that." The cards also have the power, he said, "to connect people."

Card companies will latch on to just about anything as an excuse to churn out special cards. Donruss had their "Diamond King" cards and even issued mini jigsaw puzzles of stars such as Warren Spahn and Mickey Mantle.

Topps produced cards celebrating special moments and events like Rogers Hornsby's .424 batting average in 1924, and a "Babe Ruth Special" series ranging from an image of him as a boy in Baltimore wearing a catcher's mitt to one of him coaching for the Dodgers while wearing jersey #35.

Team cards were a staple of the card industry as were the dreaded checklist cards. Another card kids cringed at when they opened a fresh pack featured teams' coaching staffs. A sample: Topps card #119 from 1974 featured manager Danny Ozark and his four coaches—what kid craved that card?

Topps also published "In Action" cards with stars such as Jim Palmer on the mound and Harmon Killebrew slugging one of his 573 blasts. They frequently issued cards with the previous season's league leaders pictured.

Fleer had creative cards such as the "Black and Blue" two-card release referring to pitchers Bud Black on one card and Vida Blue on another. A collector also had to obtain two cards to have a different duo, with one card having the wording "Speed &" as a caption to go with the image of Rickey Henderson, and the other card, which was to be placed alongside it, labeled "Power" with Reggie Jackson's name.

When Tom Seaver joined the Reds, Fleer created a "Dynamic Duo" card featuring him with his new batterymate, Johnny Bench. When Bench and Carl Yastrzemski retired after the 1983 season, Fleer paid tribute to them the following year with a special "Retiring

Superstars" card. They put out a card to commemorate Gaylord Perry's 300th win with him and his catcher Terry Bulling on display.

Fleer Super Star Special cards also dealt with Bob Horner's four-home-run game, the "Fountain of Youth" was Willie Stargell and Pete Rose, a "Dr. K and Super K" card referred to Dwight Gooden and Roger Clemens, and the "Smith Brothers" were Ozzie and Lonnie. Another card "Like Father—Like Sons," noted the accomplishments of Sandy Alomar and his sons Sandy Jr. and Roberto. Some cards in this series may have been a bit of a stretch. Consider the "Toronto's Big Guns" of Willie Upshaw and Lloyd Moseby—solid players, but hardly superstars.

Some cards feature unusual poses such as a Mickey Hatcher card with him wearing a glove which was as big as his torso. In another card Gus Zernial holds up a bat with six baseballs attached to it. There's even a card titled "The Impossible Becomes Possible" singling out pudgy pitcher Bartolo Colon hitting his first career homer when he was 17 days shy of turning 43 (he hit .084 lifetime). We'll ignore the infamous Billy Ripken card here.

Ken Griffey Jr. said that when he was a kid, "We just bought the cards for the gum and to play a little 'flip' game into a hat." He didn't even have a baseball hero because, "My father always told us don't be anybody else. Just be yourself."

Rickey Henderson's childhood was similar to Griffey's. "You just had the cards for fun. Now it's more of a business. If I opened a pack and saw my hero, I'd be happy, but I didn't really have many heroes. We used to put cards in the spokes of our bike wheels."

When he made it to the majors and saw himself on a card, like any fan, he was "thrilled. You always care. You're thrilled just to have yourself on a card."

Of course, fans collect tons of other items besides cards—the memorabilia craze is a big reason fans love baseball. Or is it that we love baseball so much, it's only natural to want to collect tokens of the game? Regardless, that's a topic we'll save for another day.

Chapter 9

Inspirations and Class Acts

Two of the most famous and inspiring farewell speeches in baseball history came from Lou Gehrig and Babe Ruth. Gehrig bowed out by giving his famous "luckiest man on the face of the earth" speech, dispelling and shrugging off all of the news about his being given "a bad break." Ruth spoke of how important baseball is to the youth of America and how they need to grow up with the game. He said if a boy tried hard enough he was bound to come out on top. He also called baseball "the only real game . . . in the world."

Everyone loves stories of men overcoming tremendous obstacles, and baseball has many such tales. Absolute and irrational hatred was heaped upon Jackie Robinson when he integrated baseball in 1947, and, for the good of his cause, he had to initially swallow the bile while persevering.

As an aside, there's a line from *To Kill a Mockingbird* which basically states you'll never understand another person "until you climb into his skin and walk around in it." Imagine having to trudge around in Robinson's skin, having to put up with the vitriolic abuse he suffered. How he managed to proudly march on was truly uplifting.

There are so many other tales of determination and bravery. There's the Jim Abbott saga, for instance. Born without a right hand, he persevered from childhood on and threw a no-hitter, one of his 87 wins. He is now a motivational speaker.

Mordecai "Three Finger" Brown actually is misnamed. He did lose most of his index finger on his throwing hand in an accident involving farming equipment, and his other fingers on that hand were once broken which left him with a badly bent middle finger and a paralyzed little finger. He turned that handicap into an advantage as his deformed hand began to throw pitches with baffling movement. That led to his putting up a lifetime ERA of 2.06 on his way to the Hall of Fame.

Monty Stratton had a story so compelling, a biopic was made with Jimmy Stewart playing the part of the All-Star pitcher. Stratton's tale was special because he lost a leg due to a hunting accident and because that foiled his budding career—in his final two major-league seasons (1937 and 1938) he had won 30 games versus 14 losses. It took quite a long time, but he made a dramatic 1946 comeback, pitching in the minors despite being encumbered with a wooden leg.

In his first game that season, he fielded well and would have added a base hit to his stats, but his leg buckled as he ran down the line to first base. He began to crawl, but was thrown out. The league then decided to allow a courtesy runner for Stratton when he did reach base. At season's end, a sportswriters group presented him with that year's Most Courageous Athlete Award. He would go on to play another six minor-league seasons in all, last pitching at the age of 41.

If somebody ever writes a baseball version of *Profiles in Courage*, the story of Lieutenant Bert Shepard has to be included. His airplane was shot down while on a World War II mission. After the crash, he woke up in a German prison hospital. It was there that he discovered his right leg had been amputated.

Before enlisting in the Army in 1942, he had posted a record of 15-21 in the minors. Undeterred, when he returned home he tried out with the Washington Senators, limping to the mound on his artificial leg. With the war still going on, teams needed healthy bodies, but could this man fit the bill? Even his team had their doubts, using him mainly to throw batting practice and to serve as a model to other handicapped servicemen.

Finally, deep into the 1945 season, he got the call from the bullpen. On that August afternoon, Shepard worked 5⅓ innings, striking out two, and leaving the majors with an ERA of 1.69. He would never again pitch in the majors, but he didn't give up, lasting two more seasons in the minors.

The war also gave an outfielder named Pete Gray the opportunity to prove that even though he was missing an arm, he could still make all the plays. Gray, who lost his right arm after he fell in the path of a train when he was six years old, was determined to play baseball.

He developed a method of making his throws by flipping the ball in the air after securing it, rapidly removing his glove by tucking it under the stub of his right arm, then seizing the ball and firing it back in.

In his first minor-league season, 1942, he hit a lusty .381. Three years later, he made the jump from a Class A1 team to the St. Louis Browns. There, he had 234 at-bats, but could only manage to hit .218 with, of course, very little clout—eight extra-base hits with no homers (he did hit five, though, while in the minors).

The following season, with soldiers returning to resume their former jobs, Gray was sent to the minors, hitting .290 one season and lasting three seasons. When he left the game, he did so knowing he had never given up. He could proudly say he was a retired big leaguer.

For almost every major-league player listed in Baseball Reference there are two bits of routine information listed to indicate the way the man batted and threw. However, for Gray, they list him as hitting "Left," throwing "Left," with a further entry: "**Fields** Left as well."

A 2023 movie, *The Hill*, is based on the dream of Rickey Hill, who suffered from a degenerative back condition, requiring him to wear primitive leg braces that *Reader's Digest* compared to the ones Forrest Gump used. And, like Gump, one day Hill and his braces parted ways. In Hill's case, he cast them off when he was eight years old, never to wear them again. Despite his back condition, Hill aspired to play pro ball. Actor Dennis Quaid, playing the role of Hill, spoke the line, "When I swing the bat, I ain't crippled no more." Hill wound up playing four minor-league seasons, once hitting .350 in A ball. One of the movie's co-writers, Angelo Pizzo, also wrote of other underdogs in *Rudy* and *Hoosiers*.

In the days before even a modicum of political correctness existed, in an era when vicious barbs were hurled back and forth across the field from players of one team to the other, a deaf player was given the nickname of "Dummy" Hoy. His career, as a lifetime .294 hitter, ran from 1888 through 1902, and as a rookie he led his league with 82 steals. The first deaf player in the majors, Ed Dundon, broke into the majors in 1883. Trivia note: On May 16, 1902, Hoy faced another deaf player, Luther Taylor, who was also given the same insensitive nickname as Hoy.

Years later, the son of country singer Charley Pride, Curtis, carved out an 11-year big-league career despite being deaf since birth. Never a star, he refused to let his handicap stop him, and in 1996, he hit .300 for the Detroit Tigers.

There have been several people who despite being blind have become baseball broadcasters. In 1989, Mike Veeck's New Britain Red Sox hired Don Wardlow, a man born with no eyes, to provide color commentary for their games. He did his prep homework by devouring a never-ending amount of stats and info from a machine that took the data and transformed it into Braille printouts.

A prime example of one man who paid his dues over and over again by first toiling in the relatively obscure Negro Leagues and in countless barnstorming games is Satchel Paige. He labored far from the brilliant glare of big-league lamps before becoming the oldest man ever to break into the majors.

Likewise, Jim Morris, the subject of a Disney movie, was far removed from diapers when he got his first shot in the majors. His debut with Tampa Bay came when he was 35, some 10 years after he walked away from pro ball and became a high school physics teacher. When he coached high school ball in 1999, his players, seeing him fire some impressive fastballs, encouraged him to attempt a comeback.

He went to a tryout camp in mid-June of 1999, hit 98 on the radar gun, up 12 mph from his speed of 10 years earlier, and he got a September callup, striking out the first man he faced. It was a whirlwind year, going from the classroom to big-league diamonds in less than three months after signing with the Devil Rays.

The award for patience goes to Dave Maggi. This third baseman played an interminable 13 minor-league seasons and 1,183 games covering 4,602 plate appearances before stepping into a big-league batter's box. In 2023, at the age of 34, the Pirates played him in three April contests. He went 2-for-6. He had made the grade.

Adam Greenberg's story of making it is both happy and sad, almost tragic. After playing for six clubs in the Cubs farm system starting in 2002, the Cubs called him up in 2005. On July 9 he was sent to the plate as a pinch-hitter. His first big-league plate appearance—just picture how elated he must have been. That was quickly snuffed out when, *on the very first big-league pitch he ever saw*—he was hit in the head by a 92 mph fastball, suffering a compound skull fracture. That led to him suffering from vertigo, double vision, and bouts of headaches and nausea.

The Cubs released him four months later. He then languished in the minors through 2011. He would have been one of only two major leaguers to be hit by a pitch in their only plate appearance and never once play the field. That dreary distinction ended when he was signed to a one-day contract in 2012, setting up another plate appearance arranged as a sentimental gesture by the Miami Marlins after being triggered by a petition initiated by a Cubs fan.

Strolling to the plate he was accompanied by the Aerosmith song "Dream On." While he did strike out as a pinch-hitter, that didn't take away from his moment which he called magical. Topps even commemorated the occasion by putting out a special 2013 card on Greenberg.

That appeared to be the sad, ironic ending of his career, as he played no more in 2012. However, his love of the game resulted in him returning to the minors to play for a Bridgeport, Connecticut, team in the Independent League in 2013, about as low as one can get on organized baseball's totem pole. He spent 30 more games there and played in that year's World Baseball Classic for Team Israel to close the book on Greenberg for good, but what a story!

Babe Ruth's daughter Julia pointed out some facets of her father that were rather inspirational, portraying how a legend could also be a good father as well as being modest despite stardom.

She said she was most proud of being Babe's daughter not because of what he accomplished on the field, but rather "just for him being the person that he was and for being such a wonderful father. There aren't a lot of stepfathers, which, of course, he started out as, who adopt the children that they are a stepfather to. He treated me as if I had always been his and I never knew another father. Boy, I'm telling you something, I just thought, and I still do think, that I was the luckiest girl in the world to have him adopt me; he was just so wonderful."

She said she didn't even *care* that he was a superstar ballplayer. "Absolutely. It wouldn't have changed what he was." In fact, Babe "pretty much left it [his achievements] on the field. He really didn't talk much about games. One thing he would say if they lost a game. He'd say, 'I think we could have won that game if such and such a thing had been done, if they'd removed a pitcher' or something like that. Outside of that, he didn't really bring the game home."

Even if, say, the Babe had hit three homers in a game, he didn't discuss it. As Julia noted, "It wasn't as if he hadn't done it before. When he hit the last three in Pittsburgh, Mother was with him. I wasn't, but I thought it was great. To me it was Daddy and that was the kind of thing that Daddy did."

She felt her father was also honorable. "I, along with Mother, do wish that he had retired after that, but when he made a promise, he kept it no matter what, and he had promised [team owner] Judge Fuchs that he would finish the particular trip until they got back to Boston—that was when he handed in his retirement."

Dave Dravecky's situation made him the center of baseball fans' attention everywhere. In September of 1988, a cancerous tumor was discovered in his left (pitching) arm, and surgery soon followed. It took until August of the next year before he could return to the Giants starting rotation.

In his first outing, he went eight innings and got the win after giving up just four hits and three runs. Touchingly, when he had begun to warm up prior to the game, fans near the bullpen began to clap. Moments later, the entire crowd of 34,810 fans gave him a standing ovation. At the end of each inning which he pitched, the crowd continued to give him standing ovations.

His next start, though, would be his last one ever. He pitched five innings and gave up two runs, but in that contest he broke his left arm while unleashing a wild pitch. The sickening sound of the bone snapping could be heard throughout the park—one witness compared the sound to that of a firecracker. Dravecky's cancer had returned. Sadly, he retired at season's end and later had to have the arm amputated. He also had his collarbone and shoulder blade removed to stop the cancer and a staph infection.

His devotion to the game was as commendable as it was inspirational. It also turned one particular seasoned veteran, Brett Butler, into a fan, and a sentimental fan at that. Looking back, he said, "The most incredible thing [I ever encountered] was to see a modern miracle happen. It was August 10 of 1989, when Dave Dravecky came back from the doctors saying he'd never pitch again. He'd lost almost three-quarters of his deltoid. They said he wouldn't even be able to take a wad out of his back pocket.

"Then, between him and Steve Bedrosian, they threw a four-hitter against the Cincinnati Reds, and I was in center field. It was a big emotional moment because they said it wouldn't happen, and he defied the odds and went out and did it." Such stories touch your heart and linger there forever, and are yet further reasons to love baseball.

By the same token, the sad tale of Andre Thornton became a story of overcoming tragedy through faith. He grew up in the 1950s with a devout mother, but his youth, spent in a rough neighborhood, was far removed from an idealized "Leave It to Beaver" world. His father had a drinking problem, giving his family a "turbulent environment."

His tribulations reached a peak when he lost his wife, Gert, and daughter in a car crash not long after his 1977 season with Cleveland. The family was traveling back to Gert's hometown so she could be a bridesmaid in her sister's wedding. Their late-night ride was rough, as they fought their way through snow mixed with freezing rain. When a blast of arctic wind smacked their vehicle, it slid and crashed into the guardrail.

When Andre was being driven to a relative's house, he glanced out the window and saw a hearse traveling in the other direction. In his autobiography, *Triumph Born of Tragedy*, he wrote, "My emotions, somewhat controlled until then, snapped, and I wept, knowing that this vehicle was going to pick up the bodies of my two loved ones." His wife and daughter were placed together in one coffin and Andre had to comfort his terrified son, Andy.

Somehow, Andre found the will to carry on, and he said, "God had left us on earth for a purpose." A friend of Thornton's called him a man "more interested in getting people a home in heaven" than anything he could achieve on a diamond.

Thornton's main goal in life became spreading the word of God, and one of his messages seemed to ring out that if he could live through such a tragedy and still see the aftermath as "a triumph," everyone should find hope in life and strive to "reach the highest goals they can, and to realize God has put them here for that purpose."

Selfless pitchers can evoke feelings of admiration and motivate their peers. Southpaw Jamie Moyer spent a quarter of a century in a major-league uniform. During one of those seasons, he was on a staff whose relief corps had been badly overworked and therefore was desperately in need of some rest. He took to the mound thinking he had to give his team seven innings or so. Instead, he got shelled from the outset of the game.

Realizing his team was probably going to lose anyway, he sucked it up, stuck it out for well over 100 pitches, and absorbed a beating which hurt not merely his record, but his earned run average as well. Bob Brenly, who led his Diamondbacks to the world championship in his first season as a manager, commented, "There's a lot more of it [playing and sacrificing for the team] than you would imagine." However, he added, "I don't know if I could put a percentage on it, but I've been around this game a long time and the guys who care more about their stats than their team winning are definitely in a minority—a small minority."

Tragedy struck umpire Steve Palermo in 1991 when he was shot while trying to break up a robbery. It was a case of a nice man being in the wrong place at the wrong time as he happened to be near the parking lot of a Dallas restaurant when two waitresses were being mugged. He was helping the victims and chasing one of the muggers when another one of the criminals shot Palermo. His spinal cord injured, his career was over, but that was not the end of his story.

Through taxing rehabilitation, he recovered, able to walk again with the help of a cane. Then, before the first game of the 1991 World Series, baseball honored him by having him throw out the first pitch. He went on to become supervisor of big-league umpires.

Such determination is an admired quality. Bobby Bragan managed such stars as Roberto Clemente, Hank Aaron, Tommie Davis, and Maury Wills, but he said "Frank Robinson was the best hitter I ever saw after a knockdown. He was up in the batter's box after a knockdown and the pitcher wasn't ready to pitch, but Frank was ready for him.

"We were playing Cincinnati a doubleheader and Eddie Mathews, who was very scrappy, was playing third base and Robinson slid into third base—it was kind of a rough slide—and they threw fists at each other. Robinson got a black eye and Mathews got a lump on his chin. In the second game Robinson hit two home runs with one eye, that's how great he was." That type of play spurs teammates on.

A mascot, of all people, served as a refreshing inspiration to those who feel as if America has become too litigious, too greedy, too ready to try to cash in on virtually anything.

In 2003, Mandy Block was a 19-year-old college student working for the Milwaukee Brewers earning $7 an hour. One of her duties was to act as the Italian Sausage in the team's traditional seventh-inning stretch Sausage Race. On July 9, as she darted around the field and neared the visiting dugout, Pittsburgh's Randall Simon playfully took a swing at Block inside her eight-foot costume. He connected and she fell, fortunately suffering only a scraped knee.

Chicago Tribune writer Rick Morrissey stated, "We all know people who would sue at the drop of a bat. But Block was no ordinary Italian Sausage." She, he wrote, had common sense, refreshingly refusing to take legal action, although she said she knew "of people taking huge advantage of situations like this and making lots of money."

Police handcuffed and arrested Simon for disorderly conduct (at first for battery), and fined him $432, and while he was suspended by MLB for three games and fined another $2,000, Block was satisfied with a Simon apology and his giving her "the offending bat" which he autographed. She commented, "I thought [not suing] was the thing you were supposed to do. Why would I sue?" Very refreshing.

Ideally, baseball is colorblind. In 1971, Danny Murtaugh fielded a starting lineup of Black and Latino players at every position, including Willie Stargell and Clemente. And, on Roberto Clemente Day in 2022, the Tampa Bay Rays nine starting batters were all Latinos, hailing from five different countries.

Ted Williams had uplifting words to heed. "Baseball gives every American boy a chance to excel, not just be as good as somebody else but to be better than somebody else." He also observed, "Baseball is the only field of endeavor where a man can succeed three times out of ten and be considered a good performer [a .300 hitter]."

Fred Wilcox, an investment manager, used a baseball metaphor to make the point that progress will always involve risk. "You can't steal second base and keep one foot on first."

We love baseball because of its many class acts. Take, for example, a sampling of some winners of the Roberto Clemente Award which is given annually to a player who demonstrates the values which Clemente "displayed in his commitment to community and understanding the value of helping others." The list includes Craig Biggio, Jamie Moyer, Cal Ripken Jr., Ozzie Smith, Willie Stargell, Al Kaline, Curtis Granderson, Brooks Robinson, Andrew McCutchen, Clayton Kershaw, and the very first recipient of the award, Willie Mays in 1971.

Likewise, Stan Musial personifies the concept of class and geniality. He was probably the most fan-friendly star of them all. In the book *Stan the Man: The Life and Times of Stan Musial*, world famous trumpeter Al Hirt noted Musial's loyalty to youngsters and his willingness to sign autographs. "No matter what he's doing, he stops."

George F. Will called Musial "an extraordinarily affable man. It was like he was Everyman, except, and this is what you have to keep in mind, no one gets to be that good in athletics by being a normal man." And Cardinals teammate Marty Marion summed Musial up by saying, "Stan was just a good ol' country boy . . . No, if you didn't like Stan, you didn't like anybody."

A few other class acts I've had the privilege of dealing with include: Johnny Oates, Buck Showalter, Herbert Perry, Carl Erskine, Vinny Castilla, Hal Smith, Billy Wagner, Troy Percival, Omar Vizquel, Jeff Francoeur, Rusty Staub, Jesse Orosco, Kent Tekulve, Curtis Granderson, John Olerud, Stu Miller, Ralph Terry, Mike Garcia, Johnny Damon, Sam Jethroe, and Andy Van Slyke.

Bust of Stan Musial, baseball legend and one of the most fan-friendly and genial sports figures ever. COURTESY OF THE LIBRARY OF CONGRESS

Among the friendliest and most cooperative Hall of Famers were Ozzie Smith, Alan Trammell, Nolan Ryan, Lee Smith, Trevor Hoffman, Goose Gossage, Joe Torre, and Sparky Anderson. All of them are reasons to love baseball (hope some of your favorites were listed).

Chapter 10

Ballparks' Traditions and Quirks

Every ballpark ever erected going back to the first official, fully enclosed park, Union Grounds (1862), has its own characteristics—like fingerprints and snowflakes, no two are alike. The dimensions and layouts of the venues, the traditions, and the quirks (such as some ballparks which had a section of sloped, not level, outfields) of the parks make them unique. This chapter covers some, but far from all, of these special ballparks. Sidenote: Elysian Fields is considered by many to be baseball's first park, or at least the birthplace of baseball, with its first game taking place on June 19, 1846.

Traditions

Over time, most ballparks and their teams develop their own traditions (or have ones thrust upon them). From rally caps used to encourage the Texas Rangers to the Tomahawk Chop of Braves fans at the "Chop Shop" in Atlanta, fans find many ways to root for their favorite teams. As an aside: All-Star Johnny Damon dismissed one tradition's origin when he said that the rally cap "goes all the way back to playground ball, you can't pin it down to a team."

One team's most long-standing tradition dated back well before the seventh-inning stretch. Having the Cincinnati Reds host the very first big-league game of a new season was something to count on almost every single season dating back to 1876.

Writer Tom Boswell came up with the phrase "time begins on Opening Day," and that was so true in the Queen City which, among other things, celebrates baseball's version of a Happy New Year with its annual Findlay Market Opening Day Parade packed full of bands, floats, and more than 170 marching groups. It's a delightful day for kids as some schools shut down for the day.

For an eon, Wrigley Field enjoyed the tradition of playing only day games, a sort of baseball lifestyle which lasted until 1988. Prior to Wrigley Field, the last park of the original 16 major-league clubs to add lights, allowing them to play night contests, was Tiger Stadium,

The Friendly Confines of Wrigley Field, a ballpark steeped in tradition, a true gem

and they did that 40 years earlier than the Cubs. Thus, the Cubs had a stranglehold on the day-games-only tradition for two generations.

If an opposing player homers into the bleachers, Cubs fans, even those tempted to keep a souvenir, disdainfully throw the ball onto the field, often while being serenaded by a bleacher chorus of, "Throw it back! Throw it back!"

Once, in a different ballpark a copycat fan threw a home-run ball back and police escorted him out of the facility since the fan was guilty of violating a rule stating spectators are *not* to throw objects onto the field. The cops could've scolded him, paraphrasing a line from *The Wizard of Oz*, "You're not in Chicago anymore."

One time a 65-year-old fan named Mike Pullin must have had the gift of foresight. Perhaps being a bit greedy, he took an old, battered ball into Wrigley with him. After he caught a home-run ball he performed an amateur magic act, employing some sleight of hand to substitute his beat-up ball for the game ball, ready to obey the "throw it back" mandate.

Wrigley Field flies a white banner with a blue letter "W" from a flagpole after a Cubs victory, or a blue pennant with a white "L" to indicate a loss. Passersby, say on the nearby elevated train track, can spot the flags to learn the latest game's outcome.

Their foul poles' banners with the retired jersey numbers of Ernie Banks, Billy Williams, Greg Maddux, Ron Santo, Fergie Jenkins, and Ryne Sandberg flutter away, and the poles' screens are adorned by the catchphrase of broadcaster Jack Brickhouse, "Hey, Hey." Pennants with the names of the NL teams also fly over the park, with the flags' positions indicating each team's place in the standings.

The Wave was once on display frequently in numerous big-league parks, and may still fleetingly pop up in sports sites on occasion. This demonstration, that people tend to either love or despise, has fans bolting from their seats in unison, rotating section-by-section, around the park to create the illusion of an ocean's wave.

Interestingly, this demonstration is said to have begun in 1979 at a hockey game between the Montreal Canadiens and the Colorado Rockies at McNichols Sports Arena in Denver. Ernie Harwell stated it spread to football at Washington State, but, "The first baseball wave, I think, was done in Tiger Stadium. I don't know that we're too proud of that," he added with a chuckle, "but it happened anyway."

Beach balls were the favorite prop of spectators starting in the 60s in Dodger Stadium as people got caught up in the action of batting them around during games. Danny Goodman worked for the Dodgers and he began merchandising all types of Dodger souvenirs, and that included a Dodger beach ball for $1. Like The Wave, purists decry the beach ball antics.

In Anaheim, one tradition was the playing of a video featuring a Rally Monkey whose acrobatic gyrations on the screen seemed to help the Angels win the World Series in 2002. Originally the video was actual footage taken from the movie *Ace Ventura: Pet Detective* and, for whatever reason, it worked in drumming up enthusiasm for the Angels. They later used a capuchin monkey to serve as a sort of video mascot.

Raucous fans in Anaheim also showed their support by banging ThunderStix, also known by other names such as Halo Sticks, together. The two long, thin balloons somehow create an enormous, deafening noise, and when, say 50,000 of them are in use at the same time the result is, well, thunderous. These noisemakers are traced back to Korean baseball.

Candlestick Park also had a quaint tradition. Because that home of the Giants was so bitterly cold many nights due to severe winds coming in from the San Francisco Bay, fans who endured an extra-inning night game were bestowed with a special pin, much like a badge of courage. Hearty spectators proudly displayed what Giants officials labeled the "Croix de Candlestick."

Sometimes a single fan creates a tradition and gains a degree of fame in doing so. The Baltimore Orioles had a number one fan named "Wild Bill" Hagy. A cabdriver by day, and an amateur contortionist at night, he led the crowd in cheering, beginning in the late 1970s from Section 34 in Memorial Stadium, hence the phrase, "The Roar from 34," and his nickname of the "Pied Piper of Section 34."

Sporting long hair and bushy beard, and with his trademark cowboy-like straw hat, he became a ballpark fixture and was given permission by the team to carry out his cheerleader act atop the dugout. Among other things, he would spell out O-R-I-O-L-E-S twisting his ample body more emphatically than is done during "Y.M.C.A." The team offered free tickets to him, but he refused, saying he wanted simply to be a regular fan. The Orioles honored him posthumously holding a "Wild Bill Hat" giveaway day.

Quite a few other individual fans, just average people, got so much attention that they added spice to the game, and people got to know them by name. Take "Howling" Hilda Chester, a devoted Brooklyn fan. Ernie Harwell once announced Dodgers games. He looked back, "Hilda was the cowbell ringer. She stuffed peanut bags with peanuts—that was her regular job, she worked for the concessionaire."

Her bell ringing, like Quasimodo's, is an interesting story in itself. Chester first made noise by banging on a frying pan with an iron ladle and by bellowing out her views on players and games. When her doctor said she was forbidden to shout after she had suffered a heart attack, she adapted by ringing a brass cowbell.

If Hilda loved a player, that man was a god. If, on the other hand, she detested a visitor, that player would've been wise to pack his ears with thick cotton balls.

The most mind-reeling episode involving Chester took place when Leo Durocher was in the middle of managing a game and his center fielder, Pete Reiser, handed him a note which read, "Get [Hugh] Casey hot [warm him up]. [Whit] Wyatt's losing it." Durocher resented the interference, but assuming the note was from the meddling team president Larry McPhail, he obeyed. Not long after Durocher read the note, Wyatt, who actually was doing well on the mound, surrendered a hit, prompting Durocher to reluctantly lift him for Casey. His mound stint was a bit shaky, but Casey did nail down the Brooklyn win.

It wasn't until later that Durocher discovered it was Chester who had written the note and passed it on to Reiser with instructions to give it to the manager. This, then, was a strange case of a fan actually taking part in a managerial decision at the big-league level.

Another Brooklyn fan of renown was restaurant owner Jack Pierce, who was almost obsessive in his admiration of one player. Harwell said, "Cookie Lavagetto was his hero. He bought these helium balloons that he'd send up in the sky for Cookie all the time, with 'Cookie' written on them."

A SABR story by William G. Nicholson told of how Pierce faithfully showed up at games and purchased 10 box seats. He would unfurl a "Cookie" banner and place it on the visitors' dugout before inflating his balloons. He often shouted, "Cookie," as he popped some balloons.

Harwell continued, "We had a lot of traditions. We had the Brooklyn Sym-Phony," he said, referring to a multipiece, nonprofessional musical group that played tunes while dressed in attire suitable for "Dem Bums."

At first, the Dodgers regarded the group as a nuisance and they were known to sneak into the park. One member paid his way in, then lowered a rope over the side of the ballpark where his friends would tie their instruments to the rope to be hauled over the wall. Then they

Hall of Fame broadcaster Ernie Harwell, a multitalented baseball legend who was once traded for a player. WIKIMEDIA COMMONS

joined the paying member to strike up the band. Jackie Robinson's wife Rachel said it was one of the many facets of the facility that fans adored, giving Ebbets character and a loving atmosphere.

Harwell went on, "They had a guy named Shorty Laurice—he and four or five of his pals would come out to the park, and when a guy struck out they would play a tune, 'Bump buh buh, bump buh buh, bump, buh, buh,'" he said, imitating a derisive musical accompaniment that would play as the opposing strikeout victim marched back to the bench. "And he'd sit down and he'd hear BOOMP!"

The Dodgers also held a "Music Depreciation Night," inviting fans to join in on the band, and 2,426 amateur musicians showed up with various instruments, gaining free admittance. The team even held a day in Laurice's honor and when he passed away, Branch Rickey, Jackie Robinson, and Roy Campanella were among those who went to the services. The funeral cortege took a lap around Ebbets Field, too.

Mike Brito was a Dodger scout, not a fan, but TV cameras constantly caught him so often perched behind the plate during home contests that this man became a part of baseball lore. Clenching a cigar in his mouth, arming himself with a radar gun, and sporting a white suit and Panama hat, he was a fixture at Chavez Ravine timing the speed of pitches. People speculated his job wielding the radar gun like a traffic cop was his reward for his scouting prowess. For one, he discovered pitching wonder Fernando Valenzuela.

By the same token, Rollen Stewart became famous in the 70s for popping up on TV while in the stands at ballparks across the country, often at sport's biggest stages such as postseason contests and the Olympics. Spotting him at baseball games was a sort of tradition for many fans, like catching an Alfred Hitchcock cameo in his thrillers.

If Stewart's name doesn't sound familiar, just wait: A born-again Christian, he often held up signs reading "John 3:16," referring to a biblical verse. The woolly-bearded Stewart was seen so frequently because he situated himself behind home plate and because of his appearance. He wore a rainbow Afro wig and he was often in motion, dancing for example, to catch viewers' eyes. His actions led to his nicknames "Rainbow Man" and "Rock'n Rollen."

Arguably, the most famous fan to ever hold up a sign was Karl Ehrhardt—guess that's why he got the nickname the "Sign Man." TV cameras at the Mets' Shea Stadium soon zoomed in on him as he held up one of about 60 handmade, cardboard signs that he brought along for each game—he was said to have made about 1,200 in all. Each sign, usually indicating happiness or frustration, had a specific saying which often either spurred fans on or commented on the game's events. He began his act when the park opened in 1964 and kept on his mission through 1981.

Always wearing a black derby with the Mets colors displayed on a band that ran around the crown of the hat, his signs' messages included: "Amazin'!" "Can You Believe It?" "Curses! Foiled Again" "Leave It to Seaver."

When José Cardenal struck out in a game, Ehrhardt whipped out the sign reading "Jose Can You See." And, often after a Mets defeat, he alluded to Charlie Brown with a one-word sign, "Aaughh." Once, after a great catch was made by Tommie Agee which caused the fans to chant the outfielder's last name, Ehrhardt produced two signs which he raised, first one then the other, alternating them. Each sign had but one letter, an A and a G.

Unlike Stewart and Ehrhardt, the Blue Jays' biggest fan, seen for many years in the second row behind home plate, wanted to maintain her anonymity. She became known simply as "Grandma Blue Jay" and "Baseball Grandma," and her fame has spread to social media.

Cleveland's most beloved fan was John Adams, who lugged a 26-inch-wide bass drum (buying a ticket for its seat) to the ballpark and tirelessly beat a rhythmic tattoo on it for nearly every game from late in the 1973 season through 2019, and that included some awfully dismal years. He eventually became a living tradition to fans at the park or listening to his beat on the radio or TV.

Yankees player Ron Blomberg remembered, "We used to play them at Municipal Stadium and they had a guy in the bleachers who pounded a drum at every game to root for the Indians. He was like the only guy out there. People loved to listen to him."

Loved it so much, the team eventually awarded the drum free season tickets, gave away Adams bobbleheads complete with a drum and mallets, and had him throw out the first pitch. Another time he stood in the batter's box and had a ceremonial first pitch lobbed his way—he swung at it with, of course, his big bass drum. When Adams was recovering from surgery in 2021, the team used a pinch drum banger, the drummer of an Akron, Ohio, rock duo, the Black Keys. The team has a bronze replica of Adams's drum attached to a bleacher bench at Progressive Field, and they even named the bleachers after Adams. His drum and mallets are now artifacts at the Hall of Fame.

One of the most die-hard of Cleveland fans was a man whose most famous support of his 1948 Indians came remotely, far from the ballpark. That man was Charley Lupica, who was the focal point of the national limelight (even being featured by *Life* magazine) in 1949 because he, of all things, sat on a flagpole (actually, on a platform attached to the pole) for 117 days.

His Indians had won the World Series the season before, but when they crashed into seventh place, he began his effort to rally them. He climbed 60 feet to his new simple home, vowing not to descend until the Indians ascended into first place or dropped out of the pennant race. He kept his word, not even coming down for the birth of one of his sons.

On the final day of the season, team owner Bill Veeck had the pole and platform transported by truck—with Lupica still on the platform—through the streets of the city and into the ballyard. There, 34,000 fans cheered for him as he returned to terra firma.

Oakland had a cheerleading fan named Krazy George. Even when the attendance was as pitiful as fewer than 1,000, he would "bang a drum, scream, lead cheers, dance, and generally raise the devil," according to a 1982 Ron Kravitz piece in the *Cincinnati Enquirer*.

George made a few dramatic entrances into the ballpark including driving in on a motorcycle, escorted by a dozen Hell's Angels. Another time he flew into the park on a hang glider only to crash into a goalpost, on the field for an upcoming Oakland Raiders game. He shook off the collision and soon resumed his cheerleading ways.

Lolly Hopkins was a 27-year fixture in Boston, rooting for the Red Sox and Braves and amplifying her already forceful voice with megaphones. In St. Louis, another lady fan, Mary Ott, was handy with a megaphone and was hell on opponents. Harry Thobe's domain for more than 50 years was Crosley Field. There, in his white suit with red-striped pants, he danced a jig in the stands, always with his megaphone and red parasol on hand.

Another tradition which began in one park is now a universal one—the curtain call for a player who has done something special. Its origin is unknown said Harwell. "There's a lot of controversy about that. The first time I remember it to any extent was Mark Fidrych in the Seventies, but I'm sure that [Roger] Maris got one when he hit his 61st home run at Yankee Stadium. But the curtain call has been fairly regular at Tiger Stadium after Fidrych."

So do the Tiger Stadium fans get credit at least for *popularizing* the request for an "encore" from the fans? Harwell mused, "I think that you could make a case for that."

American presidents race at Nationals games with costumed people wearing oversized heads to represent George Washington, Abraham Lincoln, Thomas Jefferson, and Teddy Roosevelt (who once lost more than 500 straight times). In 2013, the Nats announced they were adding President William Howard Taft to the race, a true dark horse as he was America's heaviest president at 300+ pounds.

In Milwaukee, their traditional Sausage Race pits characters such as Brat, Polish, and Italian against each other. And Pittsburgh's club stages The Pirates Pierogies race featuring runners like Potato Pete, Jalapeno Hannah, and Cheese Chester. One final example is the event held in Cleveland which began in 2005, the Hot Dog Derby, between Mustard, Ketchup, and Onion hot dog figures.

The ballpark experience is enriched by music, with many teams having their own traditions or favorite tunes. In old Comiskey Park, organist Nancy Faust started a tradition by often playing the song "Na Na Na Na, Hey Hey Hey, Good Bye" over the public address system to figuratively plant a dismissive farewell kiss on an opposing pitcher who was yanked from a game.

Another tradition along those same mocking lines took place in San Francisco where fans hung up rubber chickens when slugger Barry Bonds was issued intentional walks over and over again.

Ebbets Field organist Gladys Gooding played the rousing "The Mexican Hat Dance" to urge fans to cheer. Gooding was the answer to an old baseball puzzler: Who played for 17 years for the Dodgers without making an error?

One day at PNC Park the titles of three songs were displayed on their giant screen. If my memory is correct, the tunes were an Elvis Presley song, "Y.M.C.A.," and, even though it was the middle of summer, a tune from the TV show *The Year Without a Santa Claus*, "Snow Miser." The fans were told to cheer for their favorite. The top song, as gauged by their applause, would be played during the seventh-inning stretch. The overwhelming pick was the whimsical "Snow Miser." Among the popular songs played/sung during the games either now or in the past are: one of the oldest ones ever, "Tessie," a Red Sox favorite that began with Boston's Royal Rooters around 1903, before "Sweet Caroline" became *the* song in Fenway; "Deep in the Heart of Texas," an Astros favorite; the Brewers' "Roll Out the Barrel," and, accompanying the dramatic opening of the park's roof, the music from *2001: A Space Odyssey*. As for the Yankees, they have "New York, New York" and "Y.M.C.A." Other parks play "Y.M.C.A." too, but the Yanks and their fans have been known to play it complete with a chorus line of grounds crew workers.

There's more. In Baltimore, during every game the fans robustly join in on the singing of the National Anthem, but very briefly, for just one word. They belt out the O (as in the Baltimore O's) when they sing the line "O, say does that. . . ." Similarly, former outfielder Scott Pose said that sometimes, "In Kansas City, at the end of the National Anthem [football fans] say 'home of the Chiefs' instead of 'home of the brave.' It's a football cheer that carries over to baseball."

In St. Louis, the Cardinals' song of choice was the Budweiser beer jingle, "Here Comes the King." The Clydesdale horses made their big-league debut during the 1982 World Series when the Cards won it all, taking a crowd-pleasing warning track tour as the music played on. After that, on special occasions like the yearly Opening Day festivities, the horses trot out onto the field, taking a lap around the track.

That Opening Day tradition goes back to 1983 when the eight horses, weighing about 2,000 pounds each, pulled a wagon onto the field. The animals are so powerful, it would actually only require two of them to do the job. By the way, there are in fact three teams of the horses, one for East and West Coast appearances, and the Midwest team housed in St. Louis.

Nancy Faust is given credit for being the first organist to play a special song for certain players and cleverly choosing and playing a song with lyrics that were tied in to the game. Starting in the 1970s, she alluded to White Sox announcer Harry Caray by playing "I'm Just Wild About Harry." Knowing Harold Baines was quiet and not extremely outgoing, she played "He's So Shy" as *his* song.

One of the first players to actually request a certain song be played for him was Gary Disarcina. He liked the song "Limelight," so that was played for him at Angels home games. Organists may be a disappearing breed as music from CDs is pumped throughout many ballparks.

Then there's the singing of the National Anthem in Yankee Stadium by opera sensation Robert Merrill, which began on Opening Day in 1967. That was especially sweet because as a kid with no great baseball skills, he had dreamed of *somehow* being associated with Major League Baseball.

Singing at Yankees postseason games, he became their good-luck symbol, and he was even presented with his own pinstripe uniform, bearing the number 1½. He even made recordings of songs such as the anthems of the United States and Canada, "God Bless America," and "Take Me Out to the Ballgame" so the team could feature his voice at any time.

Outfielder Johnny Damon remembered that in Frederick, Maryland, at the minor-league park of the team known as the Keys, "They take their car keys out and shake them during the seventh inning stretch."

Interestingly, in addition to the National Anthem, one of the songs most associated with baseball is one of the oldest songs on that topic. It's "Take Me Out to the Ballgame," which was composed in 1908 (and first played at a game in 1934) by Jack Norworth and Albert Von Tilzer. Ironically, Norworth had never attended a major-league game before writing the lyrics, yet captured much of the essence of the ballpark experience.

Of course those two men had no way of knowing that many years later a man with a gravelly, off-key voice would take that song, which was already a tradition, and boost its popularity (especially with the help of nationwide cable broadcasts). That man was broadcaster Harry Caray, but what many fans don't realize is how and where his belting out that tune began—and, no, it wasn't in the home park of the Chicago Cubs.

The owner of the crosstown White Sox, Bill Veeck, came up with the idea. He knew Caray couldn't carry a tune with a forklift, but he felt that was good because no fan hearing Caray croon would be intimidated—sure enough, they soon joined in and a tradition was born.

All-Star Gregg Jefferies said that all in all, the most famous ballpark tradition was "Harry Caray singing during the seventh inning stretch." Who can forget a line he altered a bit from the original lyrics: "For it's root, root, root for the Cubbies." Caray's tradition has lived on well after his passing in 1998. Plus, the melody sounds pretty good whether it's coming from the guy or girl in the bleacher seat next to you or by one of Wrigley Field's many celebrity fill-ins for Caray such as ardent Cubs fan Bill Murray or Chicago Bears star and coach Mike Ditka, who barked out the lyrics to the delight of the crowd.

Quirks

Most ballparks have at least one interesting, distinguishing feature—we'll lump all such features together and call them quirks—some odd, some charming. The list of every ballpark with unusual characteristics is too long to cover entirely, so here's a rich sampling.

Begin with Ebbets Field's outfield wall, which was the site of what is arguably the most famous advertising sign, of all things. Abe Stark, who ran a local clothing store, had a 3-foot high, 30-foot-long sign that read "Hit Sign Win Suit," and, sure enough, if a player managed to hit the advertisement, he was given a suit from Stark. Such signs in baseball are far from unusual, but somehow Stark's sign became legendary.

The popular and well-publicized Stark later became the mayor of Brooklyn, which once was America's third most populated city until it became a part of New York City in 1898. Stark rarely had to pay off on his free suit offer, partly because stellar outfielders such as Pete Reiser and Carl Furillo normally patrolled right field. Also, with that sign not being very high off the ground, arching, often lazy flyballs were unlikely to hit the sign—they'd either make it into the stands or be caught, and lower drives could usually be snared. Stark once gave a suit to Furillo for protecting his sign so diligently.

They say Harry Walker once hit the sign, but on a bounce, not on the fly. Walker said words to the effect of, "Well, isn't that at least worth a jacket or a pair of pants?"

The bottom 10 feet of the wall in right field at Ebbets was not straight up and down, so that portion of the wall wasn't perpendicular to the ground. The wall was shaped at a 20-degree angle, like a shallow V. If a ball in flight hit the upper half, it would ricochet one way, but if it struck the lower half, outfielders had to be prepared for quite a different bounce. There were reportedly 14 different ways a ball could come off the wall. Furillo, for one, became quite skilled at playing that wall, and with a slight slope in play instead of a true warning track, that wasn't an easy task.

Another large ad was for Schaefer Beer and the H and the E in Schaefer would light up to indicate whether the scorekeeper had just ruled a play as a Hit or an Error. Likewise, said Harwell, "In the Polo Grounds on the center field scoreboard, the big one with the Chesterfield cigarette sign, if it was a hit, the 'H' lit up, and if it was an error, the 'E' lit up."

Fenway's 37-foot-tall Green Monster has a sort of hidden quirk all its own. On the scoreboard's two white vertical stripes, written in Morse code, are the initials of Thomas A. Yawkey, former owner of the Red Sox, and his wife Jean R. Yawkey.

The scoreboard also has an in-play ladder which grounds crew workers once climbed to retrieve baseballs hit into the Monster's netting. Moving over to right field, the foul pole there has its own nickname, Pesky's Pole, named after Red Sox star Johnny Pesky who often pulled balls down the right field line toward the pole.

Harwell spoke of a minor-league venue. "In my old ballpark in Atlanta, Ponce de Leon Park, they had a magnolia tree out in center field which was unique. And in right field they had a very steep embankment where the right fielder would have to run up and catch a flyball. Later they put up a fence about halfway up, but for a long time the guy had to run uphill to catch the ball or figure out how it was going to drop down. It was quite a problem."

Of course, that's not unlike Duffy's Cliff in Fenway Park or Cincinnati's Crosley Field which featured a slope in left field which extended into a portion of center field. It rose four feet and served as a warning track. The terrace began about 15 feet from the wall. Right field was a different story—there an interesting feature was the bleachers in an area known as the Sun Deck, and informally known as the Moon Deck when lights and night contests came to Crosley in 1935.

Meanwhile, Duffy Lewis's cliff was a mound that rose about 10 feet high and extended from the left field foul pole in Fenway to the center field flagpole. The so-called cliff lasted until the Green Monster replaced it in 1934, even though the wall didn't take on that name for some time, and it wasn't painted green until 1947.

Houston's facility, Minute Maid Park, once had a 30-degree slope in center field which was known as Tal's Hill, named after a Houston Astros executive, Tal Smith. The mini-hill made it difficult for outfielders who began their chase after a long fly on level ground then found their footing challenged by the sudden slanting.

Returning to Ponce de Leon, Harwell added, "And they had a swimming pool behind third base so if the game got dull, you could go up to the top at the top of the stands back of third base and look over and see the girls in swimming suits. Foul balls would go in the pool a lot."

There was also a pool beyond the right field area at Montreal's first home, Jarry Park, and Willie Stargell hit a memorable ker-plunk homer there long before homers plopped into bodies of water in Pittsburgh and San Francisco.

"Everything's happened before, believe me." Harwell compared the pool which sat just outside Ponce de Leon to the swimming pool that actually sits *inside* the park at Chase Field in Arizona, which allows swimmers to frolic during ballgames yet still watch the games, and that area always sells out. It has a starting price tag of $4,750 (and up to $7,000) for groups of up to 35 fans, but watching a 2023 World Series game there set spectators back $26,000. But, wait, that also covered five parking passes and a pool towel for each pool party attendee, as well as a $5,000 deposit for a regular-season suite the next season.

Thanks to swimming pools in ballparks, Luis Gonzalez became the first man to hit homers into two different bodies of water. He hit one which splashed down in the pool during a Diamondbacks home game in April of 2000, then blasted one which plopped into McCovey's Cove in the Giants ballpark in September.

Beautiful Wrigley Field has an outfield wall that is unusual because it has two "wells" that dip deeper away from home plate near the foul poles than the brick wall does in other parts of the outfield. Thus, a ball headed for the bleachers just a bit to the right of the well in left field, one that had the distance to barely reach the stands there, could be blown slightly to the left and come down in the well area, perhaps even into the glove of an outfielder. The opposite holds true for the other well.

Baker Bowl was the home of the Phillies, and it featured an inclined warning track which was actually a bicycle track that hugged the outfield boundaries. The park also had a hump on the field (leading to the park's nickname of the "Dump by the Hump") caused by the facility's location on land which was elevated due to a railroad tunnel which ran under the outfield.

The outfield was kept manicured by three sheep which actually lived at the park and grazed in the outfield. Many years later the owner of the Kansas City Athletics, Charlie Finley, also employed grazing sheep to groom his grass.

Finley also had a mechanical rabbit, fittingly named Harvey after a famous Jimmy Stewart movie, installed near home plate in Kansas City. When the umpire ran out of baseballs, Harvey, with a basket of balls balanced atop his head, would pop up from his underground lair (make that his warren?). Rather than using the customary system of delivering new balls via a ballboy, Harvey tirelessly and uncomplainingly performed the task.

Finley, fond of animals, employed a mule named "Charlie O" as a team mascot. The owner of the Miami Miracle minor-league team, Mike Veeck (more on him later), has used a golden retriever, Jericho the Miracle Dog, and a pig named Hamlet to carry a basket of new balls to umps.

Like many parks, the Pirates tinkered with outfield dimensions in Forbes Field. When they acquired powerful Hank Greenberg in 1947, they shortened the distance he'd need to launch a ball by fencing off an area in left field, creating an open area balls could drop into for a homer. That area became known as Greenberg Gardens. Greenberg retired after that season, but the area remained and was renamed Kiner's Korner for the Pirates' emerging new slugger Ralph Kiner.

Another feature of the Pirates' old park was a tarpaulin which was housed under the ground in third base foul territory. When the need for the tarp arose, it was hoisted mechanically up to ground level and rolled automatically onto the field. While this device seems like a time-saving, smart idea, few parks have ever had one.

Busch Stadium in St. Louis did, and it witnessed an odd injury just prior to the start of the October 13, 1985, National League Championship Series contest between Vince Coleman's Cardinals and the Dodgers. Coleman, who had shattered the record for the most stolen bases by a rookie with 110, was a very valuable tool in the St. Louis offense. He had not only set the new record, he had shattered the old one of 75 set by Benny Kauff of the Federal League in 1914, or, for what most fans consider to be the "real" big leagues—the 74 steals by rookie Juan Samuel in 1984.

Coleman was on the field stretching before game time. The man sometimes called "Vincent Van Go" didn't notice that officials had decided to cover the field due to a drizzle, nor did he see or hear the automatic tarp machine. Shortly after it began revving up, it rolled over Coleman's leg and chipped a bone in his knee, ending his season and preventing him from helping his teammates when they advanced to the World Series.

In Boston, Braves Field was unique in that trolley cars once motored directly into the park. It also had a right field bleacher area which one day became known as the Jury Box when a reporter, seeing only 12 fans sitting there to watch the abysmal team, came up with the clever nickname.

When it comes to being notorious for quirky features, New York's Polo Grounds has no rival. Home to the Giants before they departed for San Francisco, this park had insane dimensions, making the area which ran from foul pole to foul pole almost resemble an enormous rectangle, ideal for polo ponies but not so much for outfielders.

An overhead view of the park put one in mind of a gigantic horseshoe. The facility also had an overhanging section in the left field stands where the upper deck extended 23 feet farther toward the field than the lower deck of seats. An outfielder could camp under a high arcing flyball with his back to the wall, ready to catch it only to see it drift into the part of the upper-deck area that jutted out, not unlike the situation in Tiger Stadium.

Certainly the Polo Grounds' dimensions were ludicrous at 258 feet down the right field line and 279 feet down the left field line, then immediately extending toward the deepest corners of right and left fields so drastically that dead center field was a Willie Mays footrace away from the plate (483 feet by the park's final season, but as deep as 505 feet some years). An argument could be made, though, that the layout of another California ballpark was even more absurd.

Following the 1957 season when the Dodgers joined the Giants in migrating to the West Coast, Dodger Stadium was being built. So the team had to be housed in the oval-shaped Los Angeles Memorial Coliseum. This was, of course, a facility meant mainly for pro and college football (and even the Olympics).

It could hold 90,000 spectators, making it the largest venue ever to host big-league baseball games regularly. This venue set the all-time record for the largest crowd ever to witness a major-league game—115,301 in a 2008 exhibition contest.

The stadium also owns the record for the highest attendance for a non-exhibition game when 92,706 fans crammed the Coliseum for Game 5 of the 1959 World Series. In fact, during the three Series games hosted by the Dodgers, the lowest attendance figure was 92,394.

Don Zminda wrote, "Games at the Coliseum could contain 250' home runs to left, 440' flyouts to right, and fielders staggering to pick up the ball in the park's combination of single-decked seats, bright sunlight, and white-shirted fans." He nailed it—the left field foul pole was so close to home plate, a large screen had to be erected to take away at least some of the cheap home runs.

One Dodger, left-handed hitter Wally Moon, "reconfigured his swing to hit high flies ('Moon Shots') over the left field screen, hitting 37 home runs in the Coliseum from 1959 to 1961, compared to only 12 on the road."

In Seattle's Kingdome, there was a mini Green Monster, a 23-foot-high wall in right and right-center field. Due to Seattle's location in the state of Washington, a geographical pun ensued and the wall was dubbed "Walla Walla." Behind center field at one time there was a yellow ship, the USS *Mariners*, which fired a cannon after every home team round-tripper.

Harwell recalled a flagpole that was in play in Tiger Stadium, rooted in straight-away center, over 400 feet from home plate. It stood for years as the biggest on-the-field obstacle in baseball. "They didn't bring it over to Comerica. The city wouldn't let them because they had preserved Tiger Stadium as an historic site." Comerica did wind up with a flagpole on the field, though. It remained in play until the team moved the left field wall in, to a spot in front of the pole prior to the start of the 2003 season.

Monuments were also in play, dotting the outfield of old Yankee Stadium. In the book *Wits, Flakes, and Clowns* which featured colorful baseball characters, Yankee second baseman Bobby Richardson remembered a time when "Piersall came from center field to sit on second base. The manager made him go back out. [A little later], he was hiding behind a monument that was 447' away in center field." During pitching changes at Yankee Stadium, Piersall was known to sit on or rest against a monument in center field, sometimes simulating a nap.

In Pittsburgh, the batting cage was actually stored on the playing field in Forbes Field. Bob Skinner, who roamed left field for the Pirates, said the outfield was so vast that "the batting cage was in play, way out near the 457' marker. The grounds crew would wheel it out to center field after batting practice and leave it there. If a ball got stuck underneath it, they would call it a ground rule double." Many Pirate veterans said they never saw a ball reach that obstacle.

Angel Stadium's parking lot is interesting with its 230-foot (and 210-ton) metal sign shaped like the letter A with an appropriate halo near the top of the structure. The halo lights up after every Angels victory. Furthermore, the park also has more than 22,000 square feet occupied by an artificial rock formation as well as a 100-foot-tall geyser and five others measuring 50 feet in height. A waterfall completes this Outfield Extravaganza, as it is called. Not surprisingly, this amusement park–like display was the idea of parent company Disney.

Oracle Park in San Francisco pays homage to the old days with a giant (20,000-pound, 26-foot-high) replica of a 1927 four-fingered glove which measures 50 feet by 50 feet. They also display a retired cable car and an 80-foot-long Coca-Cola bottle which houses playground slides and is featured in a light display every time a Giant homers. There's also an activity area which includes a replica of the park for use by kids during games, and a promenade which runs beyond the right field wall and allows non-ticketed fans to "knothole it," watching parts of a game gratis.

Some ballparks pay special attention to given seats. A few examples: In Camden Yards every seat is a rich, deep green except two orange ones to honor special homers of Cal Ripken Jr. and Eddie Murray. Three Rivers Stadium was dotted with upper-deck seats pointing out many deep drives by Willie Stargell. In the Astrodome two seats were marked with a painting of a red rooster and a toy cannon to commemorate leviathan blows by Doug Rader and Jimmy Wynn—respectively nicknamed the "Red Rooster" and the "Toy Cannon."

RFK Stadium in Washington, DC, was home to the Senators (1962–1971). They, too, painted seats as a tip of the cap to their giant slugger Frank Howard and his tape-measure pokes. And Fenway Park has one seat that stands out among a sea of green marking the longest ball ever hit at that venue, a 502-foot right field rocket drilled by Ted Williams (Section 42, Row 37, Seat 21).

Even many ballparks which fell to wrecking balls have left a part of their history behind. The old home of the Twins, Metropolitan Stadium, is now part of the Mall of America. Above Paul Bunyan's Log Chute, fans can gaze at a seat hanging on a wall marking the location of a mammoth Harmon Killebrew home run from June 3, 1967. One of his 586 round-trippers, this one skyrocketed 520 feet into the upper deck. The location of the park's home plate is also marked.

That also holds true in long-gone parks such as Forbes Field. Its home plate was preserved in a building where the plate once sat. Well, in truth, those who salvaged home plate took a bit of liberty with history. Had they situated it exactly where it had rested for years, it would now sit inside one of the building's women's restrooms. Of course, those who preserved part of Forbes Field did the Twins a step or two better by not disturbing the flagpole and a section of the ivy-clad outfield wall, including the location where Bill Mazeroski's 1960 World Series winning home run sailed over.

Chapter 11

Mascots and Promotions

By definition, a mascot is anything or anybody that is supposed to bring good luck. This chapter will show that not all mascots wore costumes. Many fans, especially the young ones, enjoy the antics of team mascots, and some of the mascots have even become a cherished part of baseball lore.

One of the most famous mascots is the San Diego Chicken, portrayed by Ted Giannoulas. When he was 20 years old, he was hired to wear the chicken suit by a radio station in 1974, and told to pass out candy Easter eggs at the San Diego Zoo. He got the job because he was the only one small enough to fit into the tiny costume. The 5'4" Giannoulas took that job that paid $2 per gig and turned it into an occupation that allowed him to pull down six figures a year. He joked, "I don't work for birdfeed."

Incidentally, quite a few mascots' costumes were designed by Bonnie Erickson, who once was the design director of the Muppets. While she didn't come up with the outfit for the Chicken, she was responsible for creating the Phillie Phanatic; Dandy, a Yankee mascot; and Stuff the Magic Dragon for the Orlando Magic.

Soon Giannoulas got permission to wander through the crowds at Padres games and joke around with the fans. He had no idea what was

The mascot formerly known as the San Diego Chicken, one of the most famous and popular mascots ever, poses with President Ronald Reagan. WIKIMEDIA COMMONS

to come, and said he had just figured being a mascot was a good way to see games for free.

Along the way, he appeared at All-Star Games, NBA contests, hockey games, and was the grand marshal at Mardi Gras. He worked as many as 300 days a year. In a 1981 article by Ray Fitzgerald, Giannoulas was asked if his mother was upset by how he made a living. He replied, "Not at all. She thinks I'm a doctor in Wisconsin."

Giannoulas was fired by the radio station in 1979 and was out of action until he won a lawsuit that did require him to make a name change to "the Famous Chicken" and don a different costume. He made his return to baseball, debuting at a Padres game after popping out of an egg. Some 47,000 fans watched as the theme song from the movie *2001: A Space Odyssey* blared over the PA to celebrate his "Grand Hatching."

Among other things, he sometimes warmed up pitcher Don Sutton, and, to tease spitball pitcher Gaylord Perry, he took a bucket of balls which were bobbing in water out to the mound.

Through figures available in 2015, he had made more than 5,000 appearances in all 50 states and in over 900 venues. By then he had worn out more than 100 chicken outfits and had been performing his act for over 40 years. He became so famous, the Donruss company made several trading cards for the chicken.

The Phillie Phanatic, who first appeared in 1978, may have usurped the chicken as the best mascot around. Counting outside appearances, he is said to have earned between $100,000 and $200,000 a year at times. A marketing research firm's 2008 report had him as number one, a notch ahead of Giannoulas. Mr. Met, Milwaukee's racing sausages, and the Rally Monkey were also in the top 10.

One memorable Phanatic act came in 1988 when Dodger manager Tommy Lasorda took exception to the mascot. The Phanatic appeared on the field carrying a dummy which had an oversized fake tummy tucked into a Lasorda jersey. The manager slowly stalked onto the field, but when he couldn't corral the retreating mascot, he headed to the Phanatic's all-terrain vehicle.

That led to the Phanatic approaching Lasorda, mocking him with each step by jutting out his own hefty middle section. Lasorda then spun around, gave up his plan to make a getaway with the ATV, and chased after the mascot. After grabbing him by the neck and wrestling him to the ground, Lasorda rescued his effigy. He then brandished the dummy, using it as if in a pillow fight, to strike the Phanatic. Lasorda stomped off the field, dummy in hand, as the Phanatic drove off into the sunset, again sticking out his gut. It was a performance that pleased the fans to no end.

Lasorda was also displeased with the Montreal Expos mascot named Youppi!—a name that translated from French basically means yippee. One time he became too exuberant and began banging away at the Dodgers dugout roof. Lasorda had him ejected from the game, reportedly making Youppi! the first costumed mascot to get the old heave-ho.

In 1987, another mascot, the Pirates' Parrot, also got in trouble with an umpire. NL ump Billy Williams reported him to the league after the mascot threw a plastic ball at him. His actions drew a one-game suspension.

By the way, one mascot said the temperature inside his furry costume could reach 120 degrees, and in a half-hour he might lose one pound from perspiring. And when John Routh donned his Miami gear and became Billy the Marlin, he stated that his outfit weighed 35 pounds.

The Braves hired Levi Walker Jr., a Native American, to play the role of Chief Noc-A-Homa beginning in 1969. Every time a Brave knocked a homer, Walker would pop out of a tepee the team had installed on a platform down the left field line and, as a song once said, do a little dance. Also, at the start of each home game he would race onto the field, do a "prayer dance" on the mound, then hustle out to his perch. One time a smoke bomb he set off to celebrate a home run set the tepee aflame.

In 1982, when more and more fans wanted to attend games due to Atlanta's first-place berth in the standings, the Braves took his tepee down to make room for additional bleacher seating. That took place on July 30. The very next day the team began to drop precipitously in the standings, going from being nine games ahead of the pack to being four games out of first place.

Over their dreadful nosedive they dropped 19 of 21 games and suffered through an 11-game losing streak. Quite a few fans actually blamed the team's swoon on the removal of the tepee. Finally, team owner Ted Turner had the tepee and Walker Jr. reinstated. Atlanta went on to win the division by a scant one-game margin.

Elsewhere, in 1939, a batboy for the Salisbury Indians was given his own night. The 3'6" Billy Hutt was presented with jewelry, suits, and a Ford. A year later, a minor-league batboy/mascot was fined $5 for arguing about a call.

Then there was the team whose mascot died. The Lake Charles Skippers had a toad which was kept inside the manager's cap during games for luck. After he died, a frog which took over the job also died. Gory detail alert. That amphibian died under the blades of a lawnmower.

It should be noted that a more in-depth definition of mascot is "a person, animal, or object used as a symbol to represent a group (such as a sports team) and to bring good luck." So, the first baseball mascots go way, way back. Again, no fancy costumes back then.

Take the tale of Eddie Bennett, born in 1903, who became the mascot of the Chicago White Sox in 1919. After they became the Black Sox for their scandalous throwing of the World Series, he lost that gig. He rebounded by being hired by the Brooklyn team (then called the Robins) the next season. When they won the pennant, it gave Bennett a two-year run of being with league champions.

Those who believed in things like hexes had "proof" to support their thinking when the Robins, leading two games to one in the 1920 World Series, left Bennett in Brooklyn rather than take him to Cleveland for the next four games there. The Indians swept all four contests to win the then best-of-nine series—no doubt the result of Bennett putting a hex on the Robins.

In an era of no strict rules concerning political awareness, Bennett was a fine candidate for his job as a good-luck charm because back then some people believed superstitious nonsense such as rubbing the head of certain children or rubbing the sort of hump of what was then called a "hunchback" brought good fortune. Bennett injured his spine in an accident involving his baby carriage and he became a "hunchback," and his growth was stunted, saddling him with a label that was commonly used then but is odious now, "dwarf."

After his stint in Brooklyn, the Yankees hired him and, for the next 12½ seasons he served as a batboy and became very close with Babe Ruth. In his first season there his luck brought the team he was with a third straight pennant and the first ever for the Yanks. From 1921 through 1932, the Bronx Bombers won seven pennants and four world championships in all.

Problems stemming from being struck by a New York City taxi led to his retiring from the team. Once Bennett was gone, the Yanks didn't win another pennant until 1936, more "proof" that, despite the lyrics of a Stevie Wonder song, superstition *is* the way.

Bennett's tale ended when his landlady discovered his dead body in his apartment, a living space he had adorned with tons of photos of Yankee players and what would today be a fortune's worth of team memorabilia, including used game bats laying in a heap on the floor.

Even before Bennett there was another mascot who had the same physical issues. In 1910, Louis Van Zelst, who had taken a nasty fall in childhood which left him with a twisted spine, signed a contract to work as the Athletics batboy/mascot for Connie Mack. Over his five seasons on the job, Philadelphia went to the World Series four times, winning there all but once. Coincidentally, and not because Van Zelst became ill and died at the age of 20 before the 1915 season opened, the Athletics finished the next seven seasons in last place.

Babe Ruth had a personal mascot, Little Ray Kelly. Ruth spied a three-year-old Kelly doing quite well while playing catch with his

Babe Ruth with his personal mascot, Little Ray Kelly, who once was the subject of a special baseball card. COURTESY OF THE LIBRARY OF CONGRESS

father. The next day Babe took the child to the ballpark, and that began a 10-year partnership at home games. Before long, Kelly was given his own uniform. In 1992, in the Babe Ruth Collection trading card set put out by Megacards, Kelly was featured on a unique baseball card. Even when Kelly quit being Ruth's mascot, they stayed connected, and Ruth invited the youngster to attend the 1932 World Series, so Kelly was on hand when the historic "Called Shot" occurred.

Finally, another famous mascot from long ago, Charlie "Victory" Faust (his real middle name was Victor but he later added the Y). In his article "Mascots and Superstitions," Don Nelson wrote that Faust was possibly developmentally disabled, psychotic, or perhaps both, but unlike Bennett and Van Zelst, was not "physically disfigured." Some say he was simply different—that or a slick self-promoter.

In any case, he traveled to St. Louis in 1911 to meet the New York Giants manager, the highly superstitious John McGraw. He secured his position by telling McGraw that a fortune teller told him that he was destined to pitch the team to a championship. As a bonus he would put jinxes on opponents.

McGraw gave him a tryout and instantly knew this guy was no Christy Mathewson, but Faust amused him, and his Giants did win that day. The team left him at the train station when they headed out to continue their road trip. That didn't deter Faust, who showed up again when the team returned to New York.

After sweeping a doubleheader, Faust was a fixture—the Giants latched on to the 6'2" Faust as their talisman, and without having to make a Faustian deal with the Devil. From the day he first met McGraw to the day the Giants clinched the pennant, the team went 39-9; when he actually was with the team and jinxing opponents, the record glistened at 36-2!

The 30-year-old Faust even persuaded McGraw to let him pitch in two games (two innings, 4.50 ERA) after the 1911 pennant had been secured. One source said Faust was the second–least athletic person to ever play in the Bigs, behind only Eddie Gaedel. The Giants' luck ran out when they lost the 1911 World Series to the Athletics and Van Zelst in a duel of masters of hoodoo.

Over the first 65 games in 1912, the Giants won 54 times, meaning that since Faust had joined the team they won 80 percent of their games. Nevertheless, McGraw was tiring of his mascot, and Faust was sent away, back to his home in Kansas. That's when star pitcher Rube Marquard, who was 33-2 when on the hill with Faust providing the luck, went into a tailspin, not even winning half of his decisions the rest of the year.

Still, the Giants went on to capture the 1912 pennant, but lost to the Red Sox. Faust and his magical run were through, and he died in 1915—the year the Giants plummeted from a second-place berth to a dingy position in the cellar.

The list rambles on, so we'll call a timeout here and save other mascots for another day.

Baseball has produced many great promotions and interesting giveaways which have attracted fans the way Taylor Swift draws millennials to her concerts. Bill Veeck's right-hand man, Rudie Schaffer, scoffed at simple gestures such as simply handing a magnetic calendar of a team's schedule to fans.

When Veeck honored one fan, Joe Earley, as representing a sort of Everyfan, showering him with both gag gifts and valuable ones as a promotion, *that*, said Schaffer, defined what a genuine promotion really is. "The Earley promotion was a natural phenomenon, so spontaneous. Compare it to what they do today," said Schaffer in a

1991 interview. "They give away a bat or ball, and it's called a promotion. To me, that's not a promotion, that's a giveaway. A promotion is something you generate out of thin air and make it fly." Veeck was a veritable Wright brother, knowing quite well how to make things soar.

Nevertheless, Bat Day is always a fan favorite and it's an impressive sight when the PA announcer exhorts the kids to wave their bats high in the air. Of course, long ago the bats given to young fans were functional and full in length (for a certain age-group), and not a mere miniature bat.

In Ryan McGee's book *Welcome to the Circus of Baseball*, he wrote that the Asheville Tourists' general manager Ron McKee came up with a truly interesting promotion. On Shirt Off Your Back Night, at the conclusion of the game the minor-league players shed their shirts and gave them to lucky fans. McKee also claimed he coined the phrase, "The Greatest Show on Dirt," and that the director of *Bull Durham* then used that line in his movie.

Allowing fans to bring a dog to the ballpark is a common promo, and is often labeled something witty such as "Bark in the Park" or "Dog Days of Summer." The Batavia Muckdogs held a Going to the Dogs Night. At one such event a dog "signed" his pawprint for adoring fans. Some parks were careful to provide a "poop patrol," but accidents have occurred, even in the outfield. One team gave a prize for the dog chosen as the best kisser, and while no PEDs or ballot box stuffing were involved, one dog owner was disqualified for slathering his face with food.

Bud Shaw of the *Plain Dealer* reported on some noteworthy minor-league special days. The Brooklyn Cyclones took note of the 25th anniversary of the TV show *Seinfeld* by passing out bobblehead dolls which alluded to the episode in which Keith Hernandez was accused of spitting on the character Kramer. That day, players took batting practice sporting puffy shirts and the foul poles were referred to as Festivus poles, more references to the sitcom.

The Altoona Curve team held an Awful Night, highlighted by music of Milli Vanilli and William Shatner as well as autograph sessions with the signers being ordinary fans, not celebs.

Silent Night was a gimmick of the Charleston RiverDogs as they "tried to create the quietest atmosphere in baseball history." Helping them achieve that was fan cooperation, with some fans wearing duct tape over their mouths, and many held up "Yay" and "Boo" signs rather than cheer aloud. The ushers used were said to be librarians and golf marshals.

The Rancho Cucamonga Quakers held an "Instant Las Vegas Getaway" drawing with any couple who showed up at the ballyard with some luggage eligible to enter. The four winning couples were escorted to a limo and, wrote Lisa Winston of *USA Today Baseball Weekly*, "whisked to the airport for a Southwest Airlines flight." A weekend stay at the Luxor Hotel followed.

Some other promos of note as reported by Jeff Madsen of the *Daily Journal* include a minor-league team's first prize for a lucky female fan being a date with a player. Unrelated item: The Lowell Spinners in Maryland held a Birth Night with expectant mothers winning prizes if they happened to give birth during the game. Mike Veeck, Bill's son, hosted a Nobody Night gimmick with no fans permitted into the Charleston RiverDogs park until after the fifth inning when the attendance count was completed—his goal was to have a record-setting game with no fans officially on hand. It's clear that like his father, Mike was a free thinker—he even named his son William Night Train Veeck.

Veeck also held some wild promotions such as Two Dead Fat Guys Night, referring to Elvis Presley and Babe Ruth, who died on the same date. He also took heat for Vasectomy Night, scheduled to be held on Father's Day—it was cancelled an hour and 20 minutes after it was announced, and there's no need to go into depth on his fiery Disco Demolition Night.

He did feel as though he had some winners such as his Mime-O-Vision game with five mimes standing on dugouts to provide a sort of replay of close plays, doing so in slo-mo. That got much desired front-page attention when fans threw hot dogs at the performers—26,000 wieners were sold that night. He dreamed up a Lawyer Appreciation Night for the Devil Rays, planning to charge attorneys double. Enron Night made fun of the company which cooked its books to inflate their revenues with Veeck announcing the attendance that night at 142,000 fans.

There's more. In May of 1992, he held a Seance Night after a wild idea struck him. "I was walking down the street in Fort Myers and I spotted a piece of litter. It was a flyer for an Inventors' Convention which was coming to town," he said, pointing out the town was the winter home of Thomas Edison.

"We had a game the night of the convention and since Edison is the unsung hero of night baseball, we held a seance to bring back his spirit." After that event was announced, a lady claiming to be Morticia Addams was put to work greeting fans. "We even had tarot card readers working the park."

A Madame Zelda led the postgame seance and Veeck obtained an article that belonged to Edison from his estate, a straw hat. "We had to sign our life away to get that. Zelda mysteriously appeared behind home plate after the game and strange things happened inexplicably throughout the stadium. Lights flickered and she began to speak in tongues as she pronounced in another-world voice a prophecy."

As she went on and on, fans became restless. Veeck said, "They booed because they expected him to show up, but it was 15 minutes of wonderful theater."

About 5,000 keys were passed out to fans on Treasure Hunt Night with the promise that one key would unlock a treasure chest which, according to Veeck, contained prizes worth $10,000. A Veeck wouldn't lie, would he?

Well, maybe—Mike described his "Phantom of the Ball Yard" promo. "I made up a story about a second baseman who died after a collision with a right fielder. I said they sprinkled his ashes on second base. Later, we dug him up, and strange things began to happen," he teased with a grin.

Veeck felt that baseball needed more of the fun things his father was famous for, "Bill Veeck ideas," he said while calling his dad, "a little irreverent. He had fun, though. If James Brown was the 'Godfather of Soul,' my dad was the 'Godfather of the Diamond.' Everything he did had heart.

"Now baseball takes itself too seriously. We've got a lot of 'suits' in the game who have the passion of a mackerel." By way of contrast, in 1992, he joked, "I'm 41 years old going on four."

He told *USA Today*, "I am the king of cheap theatrics. Do they work? They worked for the Caesars. Feeding Christians to the lions wasn't highbrow. But it sold out the Colosseum."

Bill Veeck's promotions are so numerous, we'll save most of them for another day, but his most famous one took place when he sent the previously mentioned 3'7" Eddie Gaedel to the plate in a regular-season contest. Try to picture this: Gaedel wearing a kid's jersey with the number ⅛ on his back and toting a toy bat as he sauntered to the plate back on August 19, 1951.

Bill Veeck, one of baseball's most colorful and innovative team owners. NATIONAL BASEBALL HALL OF FAME AND MUSEUM

In his autobiography, Veeck wrote (using a term that was acceptable in his day) that even if he ran off a streak of winning 10 straight pennants and set every conceivable baseball attendance record, he would still be remembered mainly "as the man who sent a midget up to bat."

Veeck said that due to his unorthodox ways, the baseball establishment never looked at him and his gimmicks with any degree of respect. He said that "the owners have looked to me as though I were a little boy trying to run fast so the propeller on my beanie would spin." After pulling off stunts which defied baseball propriety like having Gaedel appear in a game, Veeck defended his maverick ways. "I try not to break the rules, but merely to test their elasticity." To many, Veeck remains the king of clever promotors, the Barnum of Baseball.

Braves owner Ted Turner once decided to run a promo which had a two-pronged appeal—to fans of wrestling and the institution of marriage. The event was called "Wedlock and Headlock," and featured actual marriages being conducted on the field prior to a Braves contest and a wrestling match after the game.

Turner also gave his approval for the Great Ostrich Race, an event which pitted Turner against Frank Hyland, a sportswriter for the *Atlanta Journal.* Just before the race, Turner was seated in a harness racing sulky which was to be pulled by an ostrich. Turner was to steer his ostrich by using a broom to guide the animal.

In a preliminary race involving a local deejay who went by the name of Skinny Bobby Harper, his ostrich, related Braves executive Bob Hope in his book, *We Could've Finished Last Without You*, took off "toward the right-field tunnel gate, which was slammed just in time by the ground crew to keep the bird from pulling him [Harper] out of the stadium into the parking lot and possibly onto I-75."

In Turner's race, upon hearing the starter's gun firing, his startled ostrich also scurried in the wrong direction, running across the outfield and eventually straight into the visiting team's dugout "scattering players like feathers."

Harper was involved in another Atlanta Braves promotion—this time he was to, as Hope recounted, take "a chilling leap into the world's largest dish of ice cream." Harper, shirtless but wearing a pair of cutoff jeans, approached a diving board which had been mounted on the back of a pickup truck. At that point a truck hauling a flatbed trailer drove onto the field with an enormous ice cream sundae sitting in a children's-sized plastic swimming pool as its cargo.

Goaded on by the crowd, Harper took a headfirst plunge into the supersize dessert and immediately sank. Hope stated he and his helpers waited a few minutes for him to surface then realized that Harper, by then turning blue, needed a lifeguard more than a spoon and napkin.

All in all, though, even promos that fail can be entertaining. One giveaway idea that is often doomed from the start is giving fans a free object which could make a perfect projectile to hurl onto the field. In 1974, White Sox officials soon learned that seat cushions can float like a Frisbee and that litter on the field is highly disruptive.

Just ask the Dodgers about such woes, too. They once forfeited a 1995 game, the first NL forfeit since 1954, when fans repeatedly bombarded the field with souvenir baseballs—marking the last forfeited game to date. P.S. Ten Cent Beer Night in Cleveland and the White Sox disco promos weren't too well thought out, either.

Incidentally, nine years before the Dodgers fiasco, the Rangers held a Ball Night. When they played poorly, fans bombarded the field with their freebies. General manager Tom Grieve tried to look on the brighter side saying, "At least it wasn't 'Bat Night.'"

The Blue Jays found a unique way to give something away—they used a specially rigged type of air gun to propel hot dogs into the stands. Normally, the wrapped-up treat flew in a gentle trajectory, but one day the gun's setting must have been too high and the hot dogs virtually exploded into the stands, showering fans. Chunks of shredded meat and buns were strewn everywhere.

In 2001, the Twins held a $1 Wiener Night, and predictably sold miles and miles of hot dogs. At that price many fans felt like they could literally throw them away. And they did as food fights broke out.

The Inland Empire 66ers minor-league team bought 1,000 Twinkies when they learned that the Hostess company was going out of business. Later, they held a Farewell to Twinkies Night and shot the treat from a T-shirt cannon into the stands. No injuries were reported.

Chapter 12

Around the Horn

Baseball's Beauty

Jacques Barzun, a French-born historian, came up with the famous quote, "Whoever wants to know the heart and mind of America had better learn baseball." And some people feel that not only can you say, "Baseball is America," but also, "America is baseball." That may be pushing it a bit far, but, for sure, the sport often reflects our nation and its values.

In baseball, working as a team is a must, nine men go all out to reach the same goal. Yet it's also a constant battle of one-on-one, the pitcher/batter duel in which the individual striving for excellence is also rewarded.

Wanting one's team to succeed can also entail self-sacrifice—consider a batter who purposely hits the ball to the right side of the diamond in order to move a runner who is already at second base into better scoring position. And they don't call giving yourself up by laying down a bunt a sacrifice for nothing.

Consider, too, a starting pitcher who is being battered, but knows his team's bullpen is exhausted, having lately been overworked. Like the previously mentioned Jamie Moyer, he sucks it up, struggles to go a few more innings, his ERA be damned, just to help the pitching staff out.

Sheer athleticism is a joy to behold. Take the beauty of an acrobatic double play, especially when executed by baseball Baryshnikovs like Omar Vizquel and Robbie Alomar, for example. They combined for 21 Gold Gloves, including both of them winning three during the years they were Cleveland teammates.

And take the excitement of watching a player frantically blazing around the bases, knowing that his bid for a triple will result in an explosively hard slide, and a close call. That play, unlike, say, a line drive double play, unfolds with speed yet consumes enough time for fans to take in everything from following the path of the ball, the baserunner, the relay, back to the runner, the peg to third, and the outcome. Similarly, a suicide squeeze can be quickly seen developing by astute fans, allowing them to watch that play's several stages.

Or, imagine this: A runner is on second base with two outs when a batter lines a base hit into right field where a charging Roberto Clemente scoops the ball up, and in one fluid motion delivers a clothesline throw to Bill Mazeroski. Maz then spins and fires a relay strike to gun down the runner at the plate. Today's fans can plug in other names such as Ronald Acuña Jr. throwing to Ozzie Albies.

There's beauty, too, in a deliciously executed hit-and-run play. The infielder covering second base on an apparent steal is suddenly in limbo, watching the well-placed ball travel through the hole he just vacated as the baserunner streaks to third base uncontested.

Vizquel was such a glove magician, he found ordinary groundballs to be no challenge—boring. So, at times when he took groundballs in practice or in between innings, he used his soccer background, intentionally kicking a ball over toward the second base bag as if starting the turn of a double play. Other times he would let the ball roll onto the web of his glove and then, instead of closing his mitt, he'd let it roll up the glove, deflecting it off the heel of the mitt to his bare hand, securing it then making his throw. Pure showmanship—just like his many barehanded stabs of balls.

Select Legends

There was clearly a mystique about Babe Ruth. In 2005, his granddaughter Linda Ruth Tosetti said, "Everyday. Everyday, I hear from somebody who wants to share an experience that his father or his grandfather had. I get, 'You know, my grandfather played pool with your grandfather and, man, he cleared the table.' I don't try to understand it anymore because, like my mother said, 'The name is magic.'"

She noted that even the word *Ruthian* is considered to be a legitimate adjective. "He is the measuring stick: 'the Babe Ruth of hamburgers,' or 'the Babe Ruth of basketball.' So there's a legacy."

Once, when one of Tosetti's nephews played in a youth baseball game, the fans reacted. "They wanted him to point [calling his shot] then put it out of the park."

For decades any list of baseball's "unbreakable" records included Lou Gehrig's record streak of 2,130 games played. Cal Ripken came along to do the impossible. Incredibly, he didn't break the record of the Iron Horse, this new Iron Man from Baltimore *shattered* it. For more than 16 years Ripken suited up and played, not so much day in and day out, but *year in and year out* until his streak stretched to a magnificent 2,631 games played.

Another star shortstop, Vizquel, was in awe of the streak because, he said, "To be able to go on the field everyday is not easy to do. There are *so* many things that can stop a streak, especially at shortstop."

One final monumental achievement by a legend: Joe DiMaggio's streak—he hit safely in 56 straight contests in 1941, becoming a daily

Babe Ruth, such a prolific slugger the adjective "Ruthian" came into the language. Tons of records fell to this Sultan of Swat.

topic of discussion. Plus, he impressed writers so much, they voted the MVP Award to him and not Ted Williams, who was coming off a .401 batting average, the last time any man has reached that plateau. The Hot Stove League had to be ablaze with debates all winter long after that season.

DiMaggio also owned a 61-game hitting streak in the minors and the day that stretch ended, both he and his teammates went hitless—it took a no-hitter to halt DiMaggio. Hard to believe, but during his 56-game streak he was outhit by Williams, .412 to .408, and even trailed Williams in OPS by 43 points.

Dates of Destiny

Certain dates in baseball history produced interesting and coincidental moments. On September 15, 1938, Lloyd and Paul Waner of the Pirates hit back-to-back home runs, the first time the two lifetime .300 hitters had done that. Lloyd's homer was the last of his 28 lifetime homers.

On that same day a quarter of a century later, three brothers made baseball history when the Giants outfield was composed of the three Alous—Felipe, Matty, and Jesús. Just five days prior to that, they had also made baseball trivia history when they accounted for all three outs in a single inning. This family had a habit of turning in trivia-worthy feats.

When Matty won his batting crown in 1966, he hit .342 after managing only a measly .232 batting average the year before. His 111-point improvement marked the biggest jump ever by an everyday player from one season to the next.

As for Jesús, his big trivia claim to fame came on July 10, 1964, when he banged out six hits in a game versus the Cubs. That alone is impressive, but he did that versus six different pitchers (back when it was unusual for that many men to work in a game). Later on, after he came through with his 1,000th hit, that feat made the Alous the only brother trio act to each reach that level. In addition, they wound up with the most combined hits for any group of three or more brothers with 5,094 hits. The three DiMaggios had 4,853 base hits, while a family of *five* brothers, the Delahantys, managed 4,217.

Lou Gehrig hit his first home run on September 27, 1923. Fifteen years later, he hit his final homer on that same date. Two slugging teammates, Eddie Mathews and Hank Aaron, swatted their 500th homers on the same date just one year apart. Another member of the 500 Home Run Club, Ted Williams, hit his first homer on the same date as Aaron did, April 23. Another trivia lover's delight—on that same date, Hoyt Wilhelm also banged out his first home run on the same day he earned his first big-league save. He would stay in the majors for 21 seasons and never again homer.

One-Man Rule Changes

Legend has it that Cap Anson was so skilled at bunting, he could direct pitches into foul territory at will. The advantage? Well, at one time a foul bunt on a two-strike pitch was not an automatic out. So, Anson's strategy was to purposely bunt pitches he felt he couldn't hit well into foul territory. He could wait for a good one while wearing pitchers out. The rule preventing this came along in 1894.

In 1911, Germany Schaefer pulled off a peculiar play. One day while playing for the Washington Senators, Schaefer was on first base while a teammate, Clyde Milan, was taking his lead off third. Schaefer took off for second, hoping to draw a throw from the catcher which might allow Milan to take off and score. Instead of succeeding on this double steal, Schaefer was able to take second unimpeded, with the catcher offering no throw.

Unfazed, Schaefer took his lead off the bag, but in the direction of first base, not third. He then scampered back to first base, and was again ignored by the catcher. That was fine with Schaefer, known to be a "clown prince" of baseball, who had more in mind than just foolery.

He retreated to first base to set up the double steal again. Of course he wasn't officially credited with a steal of first, but it's said that he may have rattled the pitcher. While an argument followed his "steal" of first, Schaefer again dashed for second and got caught in a rundown, as he had hoped for.

This time, though, when Milan broke for the plate, he was gunned down to end the inning. If Schaefer made it to second base as Milan was being tagged out, observers with a sense of humor, but not an understanding of rules might say Schaefer swiped second base twice in a matter of moments. His actions were almost enough to lead to a facetious search of the record books for an entry reading, "most times stealing the same base during one at bat, two times by Schaefer, 1911." In truth, he was credited with one steal, his initial jaunt to second base.

Some sources say another player, Fred Tenney, was the first man to pull off this stunt (in 1900). In addition, while Schaefer is most noted for being responsible for the rule change, the new rule prohibiting players from stealing first wasn't on the books until 1920.

Some of Bill Veeck's ideas led to rule changes such as one aimed at preventing someone like Eddie Gaedel from ever playing again.

William Hoy's being deaf also led to a change. Because he couldn't hear umpires' calls on pitches, umps started the practice of using hand signals.

Beauty of Venues

Unlike football and basketball, sports which mainly take place in sterile arenas and stadiums which lack character, many of baseball's ballyards inspire awe. They aren't just a functional structure, they are magical settings. Some even have celestial names such as an old park in Cincinnati which was called the Palace of the Fans. It provided chills for up to 12,000 spectators (when squeezed into this bandbox), but only from 1902 through 1911.

Sure, there have been some ugly parks—the worst I've seen were Montreal's Olympic Park; the home of the Rays, Tropicana Field in St. Petersburg; and I've also sat in way too many of the cookie-cutter parks. They reminded me of the old saying, "Get your scorecards here—you can't tell the players without one." The lookalike venues (Riverfront, Three Rivers, ad nauseam) seemingly required ID tags. Those facilities could almost leave you muttering, "What city am I in?" Sometimes you couldn't even see the city's skyline unless you were in, say, Busch Memorial Stadium where you might catch just a glimpse of the top of the Gateway Arch peaking over the park's roof.

No, my idea of a gorgeous park is Camden Yards, not say, Carlsbad Caverns National Park. I've visited 36 ballparks including ancient ones such as Forbes Field, Fenway Park, Tiger Stadium, and Wrigley Field. Fans like me are elated when taking in the utter beauty of parks that came with the architectural wave which began with the opening of Orioles Park at Camden Yards in Baltimore.

The word *yard* carries connotations of backyard cookouts, summer-sun relaxation, and playing catch with Dad. Football facilities don't get called yards, but Camden Yards revived the wondrous look of neoclassical ballparks, the retro parks. Since the gates of Camden Yards first flew open in 1992, more than 20 new and pretty parks have sprung up all across the land.

A minor complaint about some current ballparks. Long ago, park's names may have often come from an owner who ran a business such as the Wrigleys and their chewing gum enterprise, or Powel Crosley Jr.

who owned Crosley Field and made his fortune manufacturing radios and automobiles, *but* they did not go by blatant corporate names such as today's Guaranteed Rate Field. You have to wonder, if a company put up a tantalizing amount of money, could they get baseball to approve of a ballpark name like The BaDa Bing! Strip Club Park?

That aside, baseball's facilities have other sports beat by a mile. One can argue there is, for instance, no basketball arena that has been described with words even close to those attributed to the home of the Cubs, with its convivial greeting of, "Welcome to the Friendly Confines of Wrigley Field."

For what it's worth, here's my list of the top five parks I've visited based on my sense of baseball aesthetics: (1) Camden Yards—love the warehouse, scoreboard, vibrant green seats (2) PNC Park—breathtaking view of cityscape, homers splashing into the Allegheny River, and the Roberto Clemente bridge (3) Wrigley Field, mainly the interior for its brick wall clad in ivy, the "well" in left and right fields, and the old-fashioned scoreboard with its unique clock (4) Forbes Field ranks this high partly because of nostalgia—it's the park I figuratively grew up in, plus it featured ivy on the brick walls, and it sported a distinctive Longines scoreboard clock (5) Fenway Park—due to the Green Monster, its age and tradition, and the view of the Citgo sign. When Joe Carter was with the Red Sox, he found the sign to be motivating, as if "Citgo" meant "see *it* [meaning a home run] go."

Honorable mention goes to old Tiger Stadium and the current home parks of the Giants, Astros, Tigers, and Phillies (whatever names they might go by when you are reading this book).

Poet Joyce Kilmer can have his trees, I think that I shall never see anything as lovely as a ballpark. I only wish I had seen some of the now-extinct ones like Ebbets Field, Connie Mack Stadium, and Crosley Field.

PNC Park, home to the Pittsburgh Pirates and one of the prettiest parks in all of baseball. PHOTO BY NATHAN STEWART

However, I did visit the re-created Crosley Field preserved in Blue Ash, Ohio, complete with an exact replica scoreboard and the outfield's sloping terrace which caused consternation for some fielders.

The Voices of Summer

Fans tend to fall in love with their favorite team's voice of summertime. Prime example: in L.A., Vin Scully reigned supreme. A viewer watching a Dodgers game on TV could hear his voice reverberating throughout the park, echoing from the sound of the radios thousands of fans took to the game. Major-league baseball was new to the city in 1958, so fans at home *and* in the park turned to Scully to provide them with pertinent information. He obliged.

Likewise, when the Dodgers were located in Brooklyn, it's been said that a person walking down the streets of the city could easily follow a game in progress by listening to residents' radios. Each step took the listener closer to the next house where someone was tuned in to Red Barber.

For years when Ernie Harwell was the voice of the Tigers, he had many colorful sayings. When a foul ball sailed into the stands, he often said, "Well, a fan from Ann Arbor, Michigan, just got himself a souvenir." Many a young listener marveled at Harwell's knowledge of where so many lucky spectators lived, not realizing one of Harwell's clever trademarks.

Bob Prince was another announcer who had a passel of such calls and expressions. He dubbed Forbes Field "the House of Thrills" and when hoping for a Pittsburgh rally, he'd intone, "We need a bloop and a blast." On close plays, such as a ball which barely missed a foul pole, he'd say the baseball was foul "by a gnat's eyelash." A bang-bang play was described as being "as close as the fuzz on a tick's ear." A towering popup was, in Prince-speak, "A home run in an elevator shaft." After a Pirate powered a homer he often shouted, "You can kiss it goodbye."

Yet another famous trademark, one which drew mixed reviews, was Chris Berman's with his staccato home-run call, especially during Home Run Derby competition. Some fans loved his, "backbackback" call, while others feel he sounded like the clucking of a maniacal hen.

Some former players elevated their game to become excellent color commentators. A partial list includes Don Drysdale, Jim Palmer, Joe Garagiola Sr., and Bob Uecker.

Some announcers became so close to the team and the players they covered that they lost a large degree of objectivity and became the type of announcer known as a "homer," favoring the home team rather than reporting objectively on games. No matter—even those men became beloved in their hometowns either despite of, or because of, their one-sided approach.

As a sidenote, umpires don't want to be labeled homers, either, indicating they favored the home team in making calls. There was once a very good minor-league umpire who worked with Bruce Froemming. He was Homer Rash—an unfortunate first name for his profession.

Again, for what it's worth, my favorite announcers: Scully and Harwell share my top slot. Next come Pete Van Wieren, Dick Enberg, Jon Miller, and Harry Kalas, followed by a few others in no special order: Jack Buck, Marty Brennaman, Ernie Johnson Sr., George Grande, Ron Darling, and Bob Prince.

Some of the announcers who attained Hall of Fame status (and weren't listed above) include: Curt Gowdy, Mel Allen, Chuck Thompson, Dave Niehaus, Lindsey Nelson, and, of course, Russ Hodges of "The Giants win the pennant!" fame.

A few ballparks' field address announcers have gained fame and are loved by fans and players. Shane Halter, an eight-year major-league veteran, said, "I like the announcer in Boston and his, 'Welcome to friendly Fen-weigh Pock.' That's one he always does [with his New England dialect]. And Bob Sheppard is good. You know you're in the big leagues when you hear him announce your name. He always finishes when you're going up to bat with your number. That's a tradition he always does." A typical Sheppard intro went like this: "Now batting for the Yankees, the first baseman, number 23, Don Mattingly, number 23."

Once nicknamed "The Voice of God" for his wonderful baritone intonations, the Yankees announcer earned this compliment from Carl Yastrzemski, "You're not in the big league until Bob Sheppard announces your name."

Sheppard's remarkable tenure with the Yanks ran from 1951 to 2007. He is said to have worked 4,500+ Yankee contests over 22 seasons in which his team won a pennant, and 13 years in which they won it all. He worked his final game when he was about six-and-a-half weeks shy of his 97th birthday.

Of course, some Yankee fans are, in a way, their own announcers, shouting out the names of the starting players on a given day. The ritual known as the Roll Call works like this: Near the start of the game a fan will begin a chant, hollering out the name of, say, Derek Jeter. A large number of fans soon join in and repeat the name over and over again in a singsong style. The crowd refuses to stop their chant (and move on to chant another player's name) until the player acknowledges the fans in some simple way such as with a tip of the cap or a wave.

Love of Stats

No other sport is as rich or as detailed as baseball when it comes to statistics. Although never truly possible to compare players from different eras, stats do help fans *try to* compare.

Expert fans revel in knowing how to interpret some records, feats, and statistics which can be misleading. For example, consider the boom season of 1930 versus 1968, the Year of the Pitcher.

Typical ERAs were reduced like the kids' toy Shrinky Dinks in 1968. Bob Gibson led the way with his nearly invisible ERA of 1.12, still the third lowest ever for a full season. Luis Tiant led the AL at 1.50, and seven pitchers' ERAs were below 2.00 (14 were under 2.30, a figure that lately could fairly often lead the league).

It almost didn't matter if a hitter went to the plate lugging a bat or a soggy loaf of French bread; they weren't going to hit much. The AL batting crown winner was Carl Yastrzemski, a bona fide great hitter, but in 1968 he led the league with a relatively microscopic batting average of .301, still the lowest mark ever for a batting crown winner. It was also exactly 100 points lower than what Bill Terry hit to win the

1930 batting title, and Terry remains the last NL player to top that magical .400 level.

The New York Giants *team* batting average in 1930 was .319, the highest team mark of the entire 20th century, and the Phillies hit .315 as a team. Those stats sound great until you realize that in 1930 *everybody* (almost) hit .300. Every NL team but two hit .300, and nine NL players hit .365 or better. Al Simmons topped the league at .381, but it's speculated that his grandmother probably could have hit at least .300. In fact, the *average* batting average for the entire NL was .303.

The average ERA for the entire NL stood at 4.97 in 1930, and the Phillies staff registered a humiliating 6.71 ERA—no wonder they finished in the cellar with 102 defeats, some 40 games out of first. Blame was placed on the so called "jack-rabbit," juiced up baseballs being used. One joke was that you could hold a baseball up to your ear and hear a rabbit's heartbeat.

Baseball statistics can be fascinating due to their tie-in with some of its strange rules. Take the case of Turk Farrell, a pitcher whose lifetime record was 106-111. Despite that, he could truly state that he was a five-time All-Star. Sounds impressive, but baseball savants know that Farrell only made those teams because of a rule which states each major-league team must be represented by at least one player every year. He made the All-Star cut twice in 1962, one of the seasons when two All-Star Games were held, when his season record ended up at 10-20.

Select Iconic Moments

There are so many iconic moments in baseball history that we'll limit ourselves to just a few.

One classic baseball moment that is carved into the game's annals is Willie Mays's highway robbery of Vic Wertz in the 1954 World Series. After a *long* run, Mays snared a drive hit to the deepest part of the Polo Grounds. Mays has said that was *not* his greatest catch ever, though. And while it may sound like baseball sacrilege, in 1997, Jim Edmonds made a similar sparkling back-to-the-plate, fully extended, belly-flopping catch that was a tad better than the immortalized Mays catch (check it out on YouTube). Plays like that are, in baseball terms, "Worth the price of admission alone."

One year after Mays's catch, the Series featured a play which is also shown again and again. In a 2016 interview former Yankee Ron Blomberg described it. "It was a very close play at the plate on a steal of home by Jackie Robinson. The umpire called him safe and the catcher, Yogi Berra, exploded, arguing his tag beat Robinson's slide. Every time I see Yogi, I ask him, 'Was Jackie Robinson out or safe?' To this day, he still says he was out. The Brooklyn Dodgers, of course, say he was safe. But that was the game of baseball, without replay. Some say that's how the game should be played."

The next iconic moment was Cal Ripken's breaking the cherished record of 2,130 consecutive games played held by Lou Gehrig. Interestingly, in that 1995 contest neither the fans nor Ripken could celebrate when the first pitch of the game was thrown. Patience was required until the top of the fifth was concluded and the contest was considered to be an official game.

As he trotted off the field in the middle of the fifth, he did so with an apparent ho-hum, workmanlike attitude. The rest of the people in Camden Yards exploded as a sign indicating the length of his streak on the B & O Warehouse now read "2,131" to celebrate his accomplishment. Baltimore teammates Rafael Palmeiro and Bobby Bonilla refused to let Ripken modestly hide in the dugout, thrusting him onto the field to take a victory lap around the park. As he did, fans began to offer their hands. and Ripken obliged, shaking the hands of numerous supplicants.

A few other moments to relish: Hank Aaron circling the bases after driving his record-setting 715th homer, a record which still stands for many purists . . . Kirk Gibson's fist-pumping act after his memorable pinch walkoff homer in Game 1 of the 1988 World Series . . . Derek Jeter's hustle when he became, what seemed to most fans, a most unusual, out-of-position cutoff man, performing his "Flip Play" to nail Jeremy Giambi at the plate in the 2001 ALDS. Jeter said his Yankees worked on such plays, but fans simply shook their heads in disbelief.

Moments in the Sun

Not every player can be the next Willie Mays, but baseball affords all major leaguers with a chance, even a long shot of a chance, to enjoy a shining experience. Anyone might rise to the occasion and go from being an average player to a temporary sensation. Some even rose from relative baseball anonymity to claim hero status.

Bill Mazeroski hit all of 11 homers during the 1960 regular season. Then came two in the World Series with his spine-tingling walkoff home run remaining the only Game 7 shot to end not only the game, but the entire World Series.

Many experts (outside of New York City) believe the Maz blow deserves to be called the most dramatic home run ever, more noteworthy than what the media in the Big Apple has pounded into fans' heads, claiming that the most impactful home run ever is the 1951 Shot Heard 'Round the World. That Bobby Thomson homer *was* electrifying, but it won a *pennant*, not a *World Series*.

Johnny Vander Meer had a losing record over his 13 big-league seasons. He did win 119 games, and he did make four All-Star squads, but going into 1938, he had only 10 starts under his belt. With a record of just 3-5, the Reds lefty was hardly a household name. Nevertheless, he was headed for his moment in the klieg lights. He became the first, and only, man to throw back-to-back no-hitters in big-league history, doing so in his 20th and 21st starts ever. Only six men have ever thrown two no-hitters during the same year (one of Roy Halladay's was a regular-season perfect game to go with a postseason no-hitter).

Now, there was an obscure career minor leaguer who did those big leaguers one better. Tom Drees fired three gems in 1989 with the Triple-A Vancouver Canadians with two coming in consecutive starts (although one was a seven-inning affair). Oddly, his no-hitters accounted for 25 percent of his wins that year; he went 12-11 overall.

It wasn't until two years later that he made his big-league debut after a September callup to the White Sox. In four games, he recorded just two strikeouts, logged a record of 0-0, served up four homers, and put up a gigantic ERA of 12.27. Regardless, nobody can ever strip him of his '89 heroics.

Numbers

Even players' uniform numbers can be interesting. Pitcher Bill Voiselle began his career wearing jersey #19, but later changed it to #96, a puzzling choice, but one which made sense because his South Carolina hometown was actually named Ninety-Six. That number even became one of his nicknames.

Carlos May once wore a uniform which listed his birthday on the back. When he was with the White Sox, he asked to wear jersey #17 so that his uniform top read "May 17."

The lowest jersey number ever worn by a big leaguer is 0, though 20 men wore 00. Of the thirty-five players who wore 0 in big-league action, seven of them had the letter O as one or both of their initials, including Al Oliver, Rey Ordóñez, Oddibe McDowell, and Oscar

Gamble. The 20 men who had double zeros on their shirts for at least one season include Don Baylor, Jack Clark, Bobo Newsom, and fittingly, Omar Olivares.

The highest number is, of course, 99, which is what Aaron Judge sports on his broad back, as does Spencer Strider. In all, 30 players wore that number including Mitch Williams, the rather eccentric Turk Wendell, and a man known for some bizarre behavior, Manny Ramirez.

Catcher Benito Santiago once wore #9, but when he squatted, the strap on the back of his chest protector obscured the number so he switched to the unusual #09.

Minor leaguer Johnny Neves wore a jersey with the numeral seven sewn on backward to indicate his surname spelled backward reads "seven."

Carlton Fisk's choices of uniform numbers were interesting. He began his career mainly wearing #27 for the Red Sox—at first he briefly had #40 on his shirt. However, when he signed on with the White Sox in 1981, he asked for and got jersey #72, reversing his old numerals. He said #72 held special meanings for him because he broke into the majors in '72, the same year his son Casey was born.

At one time if a player was sporting a high number, say in the 60s or higher, you were probably looking at a player in a spring training camp, one assigned such a then undesirable number indicating he had little chance of breaking camp with the big boys. Gary Redus was assigned #61 when he was playing exhibition games for the Reds. When he made it to the majors for 20 games in 1982, he kept that number to remind himself of the days when he was seen (to borrow and twist a line from *Saturday Night Live*) as a not ready for prime time player.

Home Run Celebrations

Different teams have various methods of celebrating their home runs. In San Francisco, a foghorn celebrates Giants homers and victories with its unique, geographically appropriate sound.

The Milwaukee Brewers once did this by having their mascot, Bernie Brewer, scoot down a slide into an oversized beer mug. Later that changed and he slid into a platform made to look like a home plate.

The scoreboard in St. Louis featured a display to simulate a cardinal in flight after their players homered. But the White Sox scoreboard, Bill Veeck's brainchild, was more elaborate. A home run there set off a cacophony of noise from the exploding scoreboard complete with booming fireworks and sound effects such as colliding locomotives and thunder. Regular and strobe lights flashed, including the lights on huge pinwheels.

Of course, when an opponent homered the scoreboard went mute and dark. Yankee manager Casey Stengel once outwitted Veeck. After a New York homer he had several of his players in the dugout wave sparklers around.

Dating back to 1980, New York Mets fans have enjoyed watching the huge Home Run Apple pop up from a magician's hat every time a member of the Mets connected for a home run. The fiberglass apple which features the team logo first appeared at Shea Stadium but was moved to the team's new ballpark, Citi Field.

In Houston's Astrodome, the scoreboard featured cartoonlike images of two steer's heads snorting fire, fireworks, skyrockets, cowboys shooting off guns, and cowboys on horseback roping a steer's horns. Their "Home Run Spectacular" lasted close to 45 seconds, agony for opposing pitchers.

In Houston's Minute Maid Park, every Astros homer cues the engineer of a 57-foot-long locomotive, a replica of the type used around the mid-1800s, to have his train rumble down an 800-foot-long stretch of track atop the left field wall. Whistle blowing, the locomotive chugs along at 10 miles per hour, lugging a coal tender car behind, but this one is filled with a cargo of oranges. In addition, a display, which resembles a gas pump, keeps track of the number of home runs hit by Astros.

The latest home park for the Reds features an area which has two steamboat-like "power" smokestacks. Homers hit by Reds are celebrated there by flashing lights, billowing smoke, and firework displays. The stacks also have a total of 14 decorative baseball bats to pay homage to #14, Pete Rose. Due to his being banned from baseball, the Reds have been forbidden from displaying his number in any other fashion such as having a banner with his name and jersey number on it.

Many teams have a sort of symbol, a prop given to a player who has just homered. It varies from team to team—examples: a Mariners trident; the Pirate sluggers yielding a cutlass; and a cheesehead crown being presented to Brewers.

Violent Action

As far back as the barbaric, bloodthirsty days of bearbaiting, fans have been attracted to action which involves varying degrees of violence. Take the quote attributed to Willie Mays (but most likely conceived by a cooperative reporter or biographer). "For all its gentility, its almost leisurely pace, baseball is violence under wraps."

It may reflect poorly on human nature, but it's true when one considers brushbacks, knockdown pitches, hit batsmen, and bloodthirsty calls like, "Stick it in his ear," vicious take-out slides at second busting up potential double plays, and once, wicked collisions at home plate between a runner barreling down the line hell-bent on scoring and a vulnerable catcher, waiting for the ball's arrival with his eyes not on the approaching cannon blast. In such cases, he becomes a human bull's-eye as was evident when Pete Rose sent Ray Fosse reeling during the 1970 All-Star Game.

Need more proof? Fans love bench-clearing brawls, the kind of fracas which features bullpen inhabitants sprinting in from afar to join in on the fray, often triggered by a hit batsman. Suddenly, at the drop of a bat, the ballpark is the Roman Coliseum and every player becomes a gladiator.

Among the memorable and most unusual confrontations was a 1981 near-fight between the pummeling Pirates and the duking-it-out Dodgers. The skirmish began when Dodger outfielder Reggie Smith, incensed at Pascual Pérez for hitting two batters, challenged Pérez to a fight. The pitcher signaled Smith to meet him in the tunnel which ran beneath the stands. They did, with teammates spilling into the bowels of the stadium, out of sight of the fans (and umps). What could have been a massive donnybrook was defused, mainly by Pittsburgh's Willie Stargell, and nobody was ejected from the contest.

In 2023, José Ramírez decked Tim Anderson with one punch after a rough play at the second base bag. An announcer invoked a Howard Cosell line from the famous Muhammad Ali vs. Joe Frazier prizefight, saying, "Down goes Anderson. Down goes Anderson!"

For one of the most riveting baseball battles ever, check out the August 12, 1984, slugfest (try YouTube) between San Diego and Atlanta. A record 17 players were ejected after the smoke of the melee cleared. It mainly stemmed from Padres pitcher Ed Whitson trying to gain a degree of payback against opposing pitcher Pascual Pérez for his bench jockeying from the previous game. After Pérez hit the Padres first batter of the game, Whitson tried to hit Pérez four times over his next two at-bats, but only got tossed for his efforts.

Later in the game, reliever Craig Lefferts succeeded in drilling Pérez and 10 minutes of chaos ensued. Still later in the game, the benches emptied again with still more players given the thumb. Finally, the umpires ordered the game to continue, but with no players permitted to sit on the dugout benches. One ump labeled it the most violence he had ever seen.

Finally, the unforgettable baseball boxing bout which seemed to be a mismatch because of the age difference between the combatants, a 20-year chasm between the 46-year-old Nolan Ryan and Robin Ventura. An article by Rick Gold for mlb.com noted that Ryan hit 158 batters with pitches lifetime, but the very last time he did that led to his infamous fight. After being plunked, Ventura hesitated briefly then charged the mound—bad move. Ryan got Ventura in a headlock and it should have been time for the younger player's manager to throw in the white towel.

Gold wrote that pugilist Ryan "rained punches on the overmatched third baseman's head." It was a case of "Don't poke the bear," especially if the bear has a wicked right hand/fist. The bench-clearing free-for-all lasted more than three minutes. Interestingly, but not shockingly, Ventura was ejected but Ryan wasn't, going on to earn a win for his Rangers. Ventura downplayed the thrashing he apparently absorbed. "He gave me a couple of noogies, but that was about it." To call a few of the mighty blows noogies is like calling a softball-sized boil a pimple.

Did the home fans love it? Paul Konerko, who was then a spectator in the stands, recalled, "for every inning after that, the whole place was chanting, 'Nolan' for what seemed like an hour long."

Doubleheaders

Baseball fans believe that the best BOGO deal ever offered (but rarely seen nowadays) was the two games for the price of one doubleheader.

Listen carefully, and you might hear the genial, perpetually smiling Ernie Banks gleefully saying, "Let's play two!"

Long ago, doubleheaders plentifully dotted all of the teams' schedules, like measles on a child's face. When Memorial Day, the Fourth of July, and Labor Day rolled around, you could could count on seeing 18 or more innings, and that also was true for a slew of Sundays all season long.

The record for the most doubleheaders played by a team during one season is a staggering 46 by the 1945 Boston Braves. That meant that 60 percent of all their games took place as part of doubleheaders. From 1900 to 1929, the Braves averaged close to 26 twinbills played each year. One more thing: In 1928, they played nine doubleheaders—that's 18 bone-grinding games, or more than 160 innings—over the course of just 12 days.

In 1935, the St. Louis Browns played 10 doubleheaders in September with four of them occurring over a period of one week. In 1920, the Brooklyn Dodgers once went through an exhausting stretch of games which included their famous 26-inning contest which was followed over the next two days with a 13- and a 19-inning game—58 innings in all. Inexplicably, the schedule maker had the Dodgers playing those three contests in Boston, then home, and then back to Boston. That's 58 innings in three days with no rest from traveling in between games.

Subway Series

Because some cities were home to both an AL and an NL team, there was the possibility of a World Series playing out in just one city. When this occurred, it became known as a Subway Series (sometimes called the Nickel Series for the old cost of a subway fare). Venue for a game changes? Just hop on a subway to the other park.

The first time in the modern era that a Subway Series took place was in 1921, when the New York Giants and Yankees met—they would go at each other again five more times. The Brooklyn Dodgers and Yankees fought for the championship in even more Subway Series, seven times, all packed in from 1941 through 1956. There would not be another such World Series until the last one to date, the matchup between the rival Mets and Yankees in 2000. Incidentally, in 1906 Chicago was the site of the Cubs versus White Sox World Series, but the term Subway Series had not yet been coined.

The only cities to simultaneously host two major-league clubs are New York, Boston, Philadelphia, Chicago, and St. Louis (don't count Oakland and San Francisco or their 1989 Bay Bridge Series). When the St. Louis Browns squared off against the crosstown Cardinals, the 1944 World Series was nicknamed the Trolley Series. This one was unique because each game was played in the same park, the one the teams shared, Sportsman's Park.

1985 marked a battle between two teams linked by Interstate 70, giving birth to the title of the I-70 Showdown Series, or informally, the Interstate Series, between St. Louis and Kansas City, Missouri, sitting about 250 miles apart, but it certainly didn't qualify as another Subway Series.

Debates

That's another thing of beauty in baseball—fans can disagree over any issue and debates rage. Prime example, should Barry Bonds's 762 home runs count as the legitimate career home-run record, or does it deserve an asterisk attached to it like a sort of scarlet letter to show Hank Aaron is still the legit all-time homer king?

Ask fans who possessed the strongest outfield arm ever or who was the best pitcher ever and there will be a fairly wide range of answers. Furthermore, the answers may hinge upon the age of the fan.

Ultimately, it doesn't matter, but you can bet your bottom dollar there have been endless hours spent on just such enjoyable debates. But they can also be frustrating. Imagine an old-timer being told that Shohei Ohtani is better than Babe Ruth. Why that's absurd . . . isn't it?

Chapter 13

Baseball Is (or Once Was) . . .

Cartoonist Charles M. Schulz loved baseball and drew countless strips on the subject. There was even a TV special produced with the title *It's Spring Training, Charlie Brown*. Another *Peanuts* book and TV show was *Happiness Is a Warm Blanket, Charlie Brown*. To paraphrase that title, here's a collection of definitions for baseball.

Baseball is (or once was) . . .

- The taste of peanuts and Cracker Jack at the old ballgame—and maybe it's also knowing that it's not Cracker Jacks, plural.
- A bucket-list visit to baseball's shrine, the Hall of Fame. Nestled in the quaint village of Cooperstown, population about 1,819, the Hall is a joyful place. Of course, during big-drawing card induction weekends, the town swells with as many as 82,000 pilgrims visiting (in 2007 when Tony Gywnn and Cal Ripken Jr. were inducted).
- The beauty of a perfectly executed hit-and-run play (or a squeeze play, a run-and-hit play, a perfect relay play to nail a runner, and much more).
- The sweet sound of the crack of the bat anywhere from a sandlot game up to the majors.

Doubleday Field and its "Sandlot Kid" statue, a Cooperstown landmark and site of many games played by big leaguers and amateurs alike

- Casey Stengel and his distinctive way of expressing himself which came to be called Stengelese. To communicate the idea of a player being tough, he might say, "He could squeeze your earbrows off."
- Signs proclaiming "No Pepper Games Allowed" in the old days.
- A hook slide, a headfirst slide, and a pop-up slide.
- "M & M" referring not to candy, but to the "M & M Boys," Mantle and Maris.
- Ozzie Smith, "The Wizard of Oz," doing cartwheels, handsprings, and backflips as he took to the field on his way to

his shortstop position. He first did this on his team's final home game of 1978 on Fan Appreciation Day.

- Fan Appreciation Day with lucky fans often going home with giveaway items such as autographed items and promotional material.
- Checking out an Old-Timers' Game.
- The right to root for whomever you choose. Julia Ruth Stevens, the daughter of Babe, had a home near Phoenix and became a fan of the Diamondbacks—even when they met up with the Yankees in the 2001 World Series! Her son said, "She took a lot of flak for that." A fan of Luis Gonzalez in particular, she believed her father "wouldn't like it very much, but Arizona had a great bunch of guys."
- Old-timers, no matter what year it is, grumbling, "Bunting is a lost art. Nobody can bunt nowadays."
- Pete Rose hustling full tilt down the line to first base after simply drawing a walk, and his aggressive habit of following pitches he didn't offer at all the way into the catcher's mitt with a quick head swivel.
- The small handful of recent throwback players who opt not to wear batting gloves when at the plate. The best of them include Matt Carpenter and Kyle Tucker.
- Anyone, fan or player, wearing a rally cap.
- Pouring champagne all over the place to celebrate a World Series win.
- Wade Boggs celebrating his Yankees world championship in 1996 by taking a victory lap, riding off into the sunset so to

speak, chauffeured around the field by a police officer while they were mounted on the back of a police horse.

- The contemptuous Bronx cheer.
- Jackie Robinson dancing down the third base line, testing the waters before making a mad break and stealing home in the 1955 World Series.
- The sight of an outraged Yogi Berra and his wild gyrations of protest after Robinson was called safe on that daring Series steal.
- The joy of stepping on or sliding over home plate with the game-winning run.
- The ceremonial throwing out of the first pitch, especially by a US president—a tradition begun in 1910 by William Howard Taft at Griffith Stadium in Washington, DC. During the times when the city had no big-league club, the sitting president often kept the tradition alive in nearby Baltimore.
- The frieze, or ornate facade, that lined the roof of old Yankee Stadium.
- The sight of Juan Marichal on the mound with his patented and balletic high-to-the-sky left leg kick.
- Landmarks visible from ballparks: the Torco sign once seen from inside Wrigley Field, the Citgo sign seen from Fenway Park, the Gateway to the West arch near Busch Stadium, the 1,815-foot-tall CN Tower peering down into Rogers Centre, and the brick B & O Warehouse just outside Camden Yards. That warehouse, more than 100 years old, extends 1,116 feet.

- Stan Musial pulling out his harmonica to play "Take Me Out to the Ballgame" anywhere, but especially for Hall of Fame ceremonies.
- Announcer Harry Kalas coming up with the fabulously incisive quote about "The Secretary of Defense," a very smooth center fielder, "Two thirds of the Earth is covered by water. The other third is covered by Garry Maddox."
- The attitude of players such as Lee Smith, who said, "I love kids. Right after batting practice I usually stay out and sign for the kids in all the ballparks."
- Watching the Little League World Series and wondering if any of the players are destined for the big leagues. After all, that's happened 64 times through 2023, and the list features Boog Powell, Rick Wise, Gary Sheffield, Jason Bay, Sean Burroughs, Todd Frazier, Cody Bellinger, and both Colby and Cory Rasmus.
- The sight of Rickey Henderson, a blur on the basepaths as he bolts his way toward another record: most steals in a season (130), most lifetime steals (1,406), and most runs scored (2,295) over a 25-year period.
- Fluid shortstop Dave Concepción utilizing the practice of intentionally firing a one-hop throw from deep in the hole across Astroturfed diamonds so that it would take a convenient bounce to the first baseman—he said he got the idea from the spectacular play Brooks Robinson made to gun down Lee May in the 1970 World Series.

- The lingo of the game transferred into our mainstream language—anything that is "bush league" is of an inferior class. To give something a try but fail is to take a "swing and a miss."
- The smell of cigars long ago, along with the smell of beer (even if stale).
- Players leaving their gloves on the field at the end of each half inning, a practice that lasted until a 1954 rule prohibited that move. Outfielders simply dropped their gloves where they were stationed while middle infielders tossed them onto grass away from the dirt part of the infield. Players at the corner positions flipped their gloves/mitts into nearby foul territory. Only pitchers and catchers took their gloves/mitts into the dugouts.
- Players putting, of all things, cabbage leaves under their caps to cool themselves during sizzling summer days (back when there was only day baseball).
- The roaring sound of jets once soaring over Shea Stadium, or the clanging of trains and their shrill whistles running near Safeco Field (T-Mobile Park).
- The sight of crisp uniforms, especially the classics: the Yankees with their pinstripes, the unchanging jerseys of the Dodgers, and the striking Birds on a Bat look of the Cardinals.
- Wool uniforms being worn—imagine the insufferable heat they must have experienced wearing them in, say St. Louis, in the dog days of July and into August. Nice to look back on such old ingredients of the game, but some aspects are best left in the past.
- Other fashion trends—including that of seeing vibrantly colorful uniforms around the 1970s (think Houston's rainbow-

striped jerseys), buttonless pullover tops, and double-knit polyester uniforms.

- The click, click of the turnstiles in the old ballparks.
- The House of David.
- Photographers (believe it or not) being permitted to be on the field, close to the action to snap their shots.
- Getting to the ballpark early to see batting practice and to watch the players take infield and outfield—working on defense before starts of games long ago.
- A vendor's shout of, "Scorecards here. Get your scorecard. You can't tell the players without a scorecard!"
- The Cubs and Red Sox snapping seemingly eternal jinxes—Chicago's Billy Goat Curse and Boston's Curse of the Bambino—to win the World Series. Who can forget Boston's improbable and record-setting comeback from a 3–0 deficit versus the Yankees in the ALCS to reach and then win the 2004 Series after an 86-year dry spell? Of course, the Cubs drought ran even longer, 108 years between winning it all, claiming the 2016 championship with their hair-raising extra-inning victory over Cleveland in Game 7.
- Eternal hope. Even an agonizing stretch of failure inevitably comes to an end as the Pirates proved in 2013 when they finally enjoyed a winning season. That allowed them to put a halt to 22 consecutive losing seasons, the longest futility record in the annals of American pro sports.
- Celebratory gestures from the old, simple handshake to the high five originated by Glenn Burke of the Dodgers. Today's dugout

celebrations are more tailor made, created often by players for each other.

- Astonishing comebacks. In Game 4 of the 1929 World Series, the Cubs had built up a seemingly insurmountable 8–0 lead going into the bottom half of the seventh inning. The cliche, "Stick a fork in them, they're done," certainly seemed to apply to the Philadelphia Athletes. But so did Yogi Berra's line, "It ain't over till it's over." Philadelphia roared back, putting up a 10 spot in the bottom of the seventh, and went on to win by a score of 10–8. Instead of tying the Series at two wins apiece, the Cubs defeat and their loss in the next game gave the Athletics the championship.
- "If you build it, they [actually "he"] will come."
- Red, white, and blue bunting on display for special games like Opening Day and the World Series.
- Fireworks bursting in the sky to celebrate a home team round-tripper or victory.
- Splash down locales such as the previously mentioned river beyond right field at PNC Park (70 homers were dunked through 2023) and McCovey's Cove beyond right field in San Francisco's Oracle Park (only Giants Splash Hits—102 of them through 2023—are recorded on a counter displayed on the right field wall).
- The old hidden ball trick.
- The bloody sock of Curt Schilling from his Game 6 outing versus the Yankees in the 2004 playoffs.
- The humor of Bob Uecker, who only hit .200 lifetime, but hit .400+ with his wit.

- Winning streaks. The longest ones include the most division titles won in a row (14, Braves from 1991 to 2005 with no playoffs held in 2004 due to the players' strike); and most consecutive pennants won and most world championships in a row (five, Yankees from 1949 to 1953). All five came under manager Casey Stengel, who won 10 pennants and seven World Series in his first dozen seasons as the Yankees skipper.
- Connie Mack, the most famous of a few managers who sat on the bench guiding a team while wearing a suit, not a baseball uniform.
- The day-to-day thrill of a tight pennant race—some say especially before the leagues expanded into divisions (look up the 1967 race for one white-knuckle example).
- Don Zimmer, nicknamed "Popeye" for his appearance so similar to the cartoon character, what with Zimmer's cheeks bulging with his huge chaw of tobacco.
- Charlie Brown being disrobed by a line drive comebacker through the box. Trivia note: Brown made his baseball debut in a 1951 strip with him as a catcher.
- Walk-in dugouts—not the traditional one with several steps leading down to benches. These were seen in a few ballparks such as Riverfront Stadium and Three Rivers Stadium. By the way, the reason dugouts were first literally dug out, sunken, was so fans could see over them, and architects knew it was more economical to dig down to situate the dugouts than to raise them.

- The first all-female pro baseball team since the 1954 disbanding of "The League of Their Own" organization—the Colorado Silver Bullets (1994–1997), managed by Phil Niekro.
- Two of the Bullets becoming the first women to sign minor-league contracts to play Single-A and Double-A ball in the men's Hawaii Winter League.
- Entertaining acts such as a Blues Brothers tribute duo, a death-defying high-wire act sans net performed by the legendary Flying Wallenda family, or a performance by baseball's clown prince Max Patkin.
- The smell of the leather of a new glove, or even an old one that has, for the first time prior to a new season, been lovingly oiled by, say, a high school player.
- A rain check, ensuring that even in the worst scenario, there will always be another day for baseball—just as Broadway's Annie knew, the sun will come out.
- Baseball is (or can be) sticking around long enough to witness both Cecil and Prince Fielder, or Vladimir Guerrero Sr. and Jr., or the Griffeys, or the Bells, or the Boones . . .
- Deeply rooted, long-lasting generational love, the handing down of the love of the game through the love of parents to children through the ages.
- Opening a pack of baseball cards and seeing the face of your favorite player gazing up at you.
- Long ago—the Zamboni machine, which sucked up water from artificial turfs.

- Pete Rose turning to catcher Carlton Fisk as he stood at the plate, reflecting on the classic Game 6 in the 1975 World Series they were playing: "Ain't this one helluva game?"
- Later in that same game, Fisk gesturing, almost willing, his deep drive to stay fair for a homer.
- A parade (ticker-tape or otherwise) and/or a gathering in town to celebrate the winning of the World Series. For example, the throng of five million that flocked to Chicago to pay homage to the Cubs in 2016 is said to be the seventh largest gathering in the history of the planet and the largest ever in the United States. And New York has hosted nine parades down the Canyon of Heroes to honor world champion Yankee teams—the last one was held in 2009.
- Bill Veeck's fan-friendly way of thinking when he operated the Indians during a golden era. He said, "Everyday is Mardi Gras and every fan is king."
- Ladies' Day, with the first one from the modern era believed to have been held by the St. Louis Browns in 1912.
- Bleacher bums of various parks, but especially in Wrigley Field from around 1967—remember the 1969 die-hard fans?
- The old joke that the last two words to the National Anthem are "Play ball!"
- Ty Cobb viciously sliding into third base, spikes gleaming and raised high, kicking up a cloud of dust like the Lone Ranger.
- Harry Stevens, a concessionaire. He is the man credited with originating the scorecard for baseball games and for coming up with the idea of serving a hot dog on a roll. Thanks, Harry.

- The urgency of any upcoming game which would, for example, decide a pennant or conclude a postseason series. Those crucial contests led to the phrases that the probable pitchers for the game will be, "So-and-so, and staff," and "It's all hands on deck today."
- Explaining the game—its rules and strategies—to your date.
- Explaining the game—its rules and strategies—to your child or grandchild.
- Game 7. That speaks for itself.

Finally, baseball is (was, and always will be) not only being taken out to the ballgame, but also not caring if you ever get back.

Selected Bibliography

Websites

ABC News, Babe Ruth Central, Baseball Almanac, Baseball Monkey, Baseball Reference, Bleacher Report, Book Glow, BrainyQuote, Deadspin, ESPN, History.com, Just Bats, Literary Hub, *MEL* magazine, MLB, National Baseball Hall of Fame, *New York Times*, SABR, SBNation, the *Sporting News*, *Sports Collectors Digest*, *Sports Illustrated*, *Washington Post*, and Wikipedia.

Books

Insider's Baseball, edited by L. Robert Davids
The Ol' Ball Game by Norman L. Macht
The Pitcher by John Thorn and John Holway
The Second Fireside Book of Baseball, edited by Charles Einstein
Stan the Man: The Life and Times of Stan Musial by Wayne Stewart
Triumph Born of Tragedy by Andre Thornton (as told to Al Janssen)
We Could've Finished Last Without You by Bob Hope

Index

About the Author

Wayne Stewart was born and raised in Donora, Pennsylvania, a town that has produced several big-league baseball players, including the father-son Griffeys and Stan Musial (whose biography, *Stan the Man: The Life and Times of Stan Musial*, he wrote). Stewart was on the same Donora High School baseball team as Griffey Sr.

Stewart has covered the sports world since 1978. He has interviewed and profiled many stars including Kareem Abdul-Jabbar, Lenny Wilkens, and Larry Bird. His key football interviews have taken place with legends such as Joe Montana, Raymond Berry, and Lenny Moore, and he has also interviewed numerous baseball legends such as Nolan Ryan, Bob Gibson, Tony Gwynn, Greg Maddux, Rickey Henderson, and Ken Griffey Jr.

Stewart has written more than 25 baseball books, and still others on football and basketball. His work has also appeared in seven baseball anthologies. This is his 39th book.

Stewart has also written over 500 articles for publications such as *Baseball Digest*, *USA Today/Baseball Weekly*, *Boys' Life*, and Beckett Publications, and he has written for the official publications of many Major League Baseball teams including the Braves, Yankees, White Sox, Orioles, Padres, Twins, Phillies, Red Sox, A's, and Dodgers.

Furthermore, Stewart has appeared, as a baseball expert/historian, on Cleveland's Fox 8, on an ESPN Classic television show on Bob Feller, and on numerous radio shows. He also hosted his own radio shows including a call-in sports talk show, a pregame Indians report, and pregame shows for Notre Dame football.

Stewart now lives in Amherst, Ohio, with his wife Nancy.